Alfred Tennyson

The Poetical Works

Alfred Tennyson

The Poetical Works

ISBN/EAN: 9783742807649

Manufactured in Europe, USA, Canada, Australia, Japa

Cover: Foto ©Andreas Hilbeck / pixelio.de

Manufactured and distributed by brebook publishing software (www.brebook.com)

Alfred Tennyson

The Poetical Works

COLLECTION
OF
BRITISH AUTHORS

TAUCHNITZ EDITION.

VOL. 1065.

THE POETICAL WORKS OF TENNYSON.

VOL. VI.

The "Idylls of the King" should be read in the following order:—

THE COMING OF ARTHUR.

𝕿𝖍𝖊 𝕽𝖔𝖚𝖓𖉈 𝕮𝖆𝖇𝖑𝖊.

GERAINT AND ENID.
MERLIN AND VIVIEN.
LANCELOT AND ELAINE.
THE HOLY GRAIL.
PELLEAS AND ETTARRE.
GUINEVERE.

THE PASSING OF ARTHUR.*

* This last, the earliest written of the poems, is here connected with the rest in accordance with an early project of the author's.

THE
POETICAL WORKS

OF

ALFRED TENNYSON.

COPYRIGHT EDITION

VOL. VI.

THE HOLY GRAIL AND OTHER POEMS.

LEIPZIG
BERNHARD TAUCHNITZ
1870.

CONTENTS

OF VOLUME VI.

	PAGE
THE COMING OF ARTHUR	1
THE HOLY GRAIL	31
PELLEAS AND ETTARRE	89
THE PASSING OF ARTHUR	129
NORTHERN FARMER. NEW STYLE	161
THE GOLDEN SUPPER	169
THE VICTIM	193
WAGES	199
THE HIGHER PANTHEISM	201
"FLOWER IN THE CRANNIED WALL,"	204
LUCRETIUS	205

THE COMING OF ARTHUR.

THE COMING OF ARTHUR.

LEODOGRAN, the King of Cameliard,
Had one fair daughter, and none other child;
And she was fairest of all flesh on earth,
Guinevere, and in her his one delight.

For many a petty king ere Arthur came
Ruled in this isle, and ever waging war
Each upon other, wasted all the land;
And still from time to time the heathen host
Swarm'd overseas, and harried what was left.
And so there grew great tracts of wilderness,

Wherein the beast was ever more and more,
But man was less and less, till Arthur came.
For first Aurelius lived and fought and died,
And after him King Uther fought and died,
But either fail'd to make the kingdom one.
And after these King Arthur for a space,
And thro' the puissance of his Table Round,
Drew all their petty princedoms under him,
Their king and head, and made a realm, and
    reign'd.

And thus the land of Cameliard was waste,
Thick with wet woods, and many a beast therein,
And none or few to scare or chase the beast;
So that wild dog, and wolf and boar and bear
Came night and day, and rooted in the fields,
And wallow'd in the gardens of the king.
And ever and anon the wolf would steal

The children and devour, but now and then,
Her own brood lost or dead, lent her fierce teat
To human sucklings; and the children, housed
In her foul den, there at their meat would growl,
And mock their foster-mother on four feet,
Till, straighten'd, they grew up to wolf-like men,
Worse than the wolves. And King Leodogran
Groan'd for the Roman legions here again,
And Cæsar's eagle; then his brother king,
Rience, assail'd him: last a heathen horde,
Reddening the sun with smoke and earth with
  blood,
And on the spike that split the mother's heart
Spitting the child, brake on him, till, amazed,
He knew not whither he should turn for aid.

But—for he heard of Arthur newly crown'd,
Tho' not without an uproar made by those

Who cried, "He is not Uther's son"—the king
Sent to him, saying, "Arise, and help us thou!
For here between the man and beast we die."

And Arthur yet had done no deed of arms,
But heard the call, and came: and Guinevere
Stood by the castle walls to watch him pass;
But since he neither wore on helm or shield
The golden symbol of his kinglihood,
But rode a simple knight among his knights,
And many of these in richer arms than he,
She saw him not, or mark'd not, if she saw,
One among many, tho' his face was bare.
But Arthur, looking downward as he past,
Felt the light of her eyes into his life
Smite on the sudden, yet rode on, and pitch'd
His tents beside the forest. And he drave
The heathen, and he slew the beast, and fell'd

THE COMING OF ARTHUR.

The forest, and let in the sun, and made
Broad pathways for the hunter and the knight;
And so return'd.

                For while he linger'd there,
A doubt that ever smoulder'd in the hearts
Of those great Lords and Barons of his realm
Flash'd forth and into war: for most of these
Made head against him, crying, "Who is he
That he should rule us? who hath proven him
King Uther's son? for lo! we look at him,
And find nor face nor bearing, limbs nor voice,
Are like to those of Uther whom we knew.
This is the son of Gorloïs, not the king;
This is the son of Anton, not the king."

And Arthur, passing thence to battle, felt
Travail, and throes and agonies of the life,

Desiring to be join'd with Guinevere;
And thinking as he rode, "Her father said
That there between the man and beast they die.
Shall I not lift her from this land of beasts
Up to my throne, and side by side with me?
What happiness to reign a lonely king,
Vext—O ye stars that shudder over me,
O earth that soundest hollow under me,
Vext with waste dreams? for saving I be join'd
To her that is the fairest under heaven,
I seem as nothing in the mighty world,
And cannot will my will, nor work my work
Wholly, nor make myself in mine own realm
Victor and lord. But were I join'd with her,
Then might we live together as one life,
And reigning with one will in everything
Have power on this dark land to lighten it,
And power on this dead world to make it live.

And Arthur from the field of battle sent
Ulfius, and Brastias, and Bedivere,
His new-made knights, to King Leodogran,
Saying, "If I in ought have served thee well,
Give me thy daughter Guinevere to wife."

Whom when he heard, Leodogran in heart,
Debating—"How should I that am a king,
However much he holp me at my need,
Give my one daughter saving to a king,
And a king's son"—lifted his voice, and call'd
A hoary man, his chamberlain, to whom
He trusted all things, and of him required
His counsel: "Knowest thou aught of Arthur's birth?"

Then spake the hoary chamberlain and said,
"Sir king, there be but two old men that know:
And each is twice as old as I; and one

Is Merlin, the wise man that ever served
King Uther thro' his magic art; and one
Is Merlin's master (so they call him) Bleys,
Who taught him magic; but the scholar ran
Before the master, and so far, that Bleys
Laid magic by, and sat him down, and wrote
All things and whatsoever Merlin did
In one great annal-book, where after-years
Will learn the secret of our Arthur's birth."

To whom the King Leodogran replied,
"O friend, had I been holpen half as well
By this King Arthur as by thee to-day,
Then beast and man had had their share of me:
But summon here before us yet once more
Ulfius, and Brastias, and Bedivere."

Then, when they came before him, the king said,

"I have seen the cuckoo chased by lesser fowl,
And reason in the chase: but wherefore now
Do these your lords stir up the heat of war,
Some calling Arthur born of Gorloïs,
Others of Anton? Tell me, ye yourselves,
Hold ye this Arthur for King Uther's son?"

And Ulfius and Brastias answer'd, "Ay."
Then Bedivere, the first of all his knights
Knighted by Arthur at his crowning, spake—
For bold in heart and act and word was he,
Whenever slander breathed against the king—

"Sir, there be many rumours on this head:
For there be those who hate him in their hearts,
Call him baseborn, and since his ways are sweet,
And theirs are bestial, hold him less than man:
And there be those who deem him more than man,

And dream he dropt from heaven: but my belief
In all this matter—so ye care to learn—
Sir, for ye know that in King Uther's time
The prince and warrior Gorloïs, he that held
Tintagil castle by the Cornish sea,
Was wedded with a winsome wife, Ygerne:
And daughters had she borne him,—one whereof
Lot's wife, the Queen of Orkney, Bellicent,
Hath ever like a loyal sister cleaved
To Arthur,—but a son she had not borne.
And Uther cast upon her eyes of love:
But she, a stainless wife to Gorloïs,
So loathed the bright dishonour of his love,
That Gorloïs and King Uther went to war:
And overthrown was Gorloïs and slain.
Then Uther in his wrath and heat besieged
Ygerne within Tintagil, where her men,
Seeing the mighty swarm about their walls,

Left her and fled, and Uther enter'd in,
And there was none to call but himself.
So, compass'd by the power of the king,
Enforced she was to wed him in her tears,
And with a shameful swiftness: afterward,
Not many moons, King Uther died himself,
Moaning and wailing for an heir to rule
After him, lest the realm should go to wrack.
And that same night, the night of the new year,
By reason of the bitterness and grief
That vext his mother, all before his time
Was Arthur born, and all as soon as born
Deliver'd at a secret postern-gate
To Merlin, to be holden far apart
Until his hour should come; because the lords
Of that fierce day were as the lords of this,
Wild beasts, and surely would have torn the child
Piecemeal among them, had they known; for each

But sought to rule for his own self and hand,
And many hated Uther for the sake
Of Gorloïs. Wherefore Merlin took the child,
And gave him to Sir Anton, an old knight
And ancient friend of Uther; and his wife
Nursed the young prince, and rear'd him with her
    own;
And no man knew. And ever since the lords
Have foughten like wild beasts among themselves,
So that the realm has gone to wrack: but now,
This year, when Merlin (for his hour had come)
Brought Arthur forth, and set him in the hall,
Proclaiming, 'Here is Uther's heir, your king,'
A hundred voices cried, 'Away with him!
No king of ours! a son of Gorloïs he,
Or else the child of Anton, and no king,
Or else baseborn.' Yet Merlin thro' his craft,
And while the people clamour'd for a king,

Had Arthur crown'd; but after, the great lords
Banded, and so brake out in open war."

Then while the King debated with himself
If Arthur were the child of shamefulness,
Or born the son of Gorloïs, after death,
Or Uther's son, and born before his time,
Or whether there were truth in anything
Said by these three, there came to Cameliard,
With Gawain and young Modred, her two sons,
Lot's wife, the Queen of Orkney, Bellicent;
Whom as he could, not as he would, the king
Made feast for, saying, as they sat at meat,

"A doubtful throne is ice on summer seas—
Ye come from Arthur's court: think ye this king—
So few his knights, however brave they be—
Hath body enow to beat his foemen down?"

"O king," she cried, "and I will tell thee: few,
Few, but all brave, all of one mind with him;
For I was near him when the savage yells
Of Uther's peerage died, and Arthur sat
Crown'd on the daïs, and his warriors cried,
'Be thou the king, and we will work thy will
Who love thee.' Then the king in low deep tones,
And simple words of great authority,
Bound them by so strait vows to his own self,
That when they rose, knighted from kneeling, some
Were pale as at the passing of a ghost,
Some flush'd, and others dazed, as one who wakes
Half-blinded at the coming of a light.

"But when he spake and cheer'd his Table Round
With large divine and comfortable words
Beyond my tongue to tell thee—I beheld
From eye to eye thro' all their Order flash

A momentary likeness of the king:
And ere it left their faces, thro' the cross
And those around it and the Crucified,
Down from the casement over Arthur, smote
Flame-colour, vert and azure, in three rays,
One falling upon each of three fair queens,
Who stood in silence near his throne, the friends
Of Arthur, gazing on him, tall, with bright
Sweet faces, who will help him at his need.

"And there I saw mage Merlin, whose vast wit
And hundred winters are but as the hands
Of loyal vassals toiling for their liege.

"And near him stood the Lady of the Lake,
Who knows a subtler magic than his own—
Clothed in white samite, mystic, wonderful.
She gave the king his huge cross-hilted sword,

Whereby to drive the heathen out: a mist
Of incense curl'd about her, and her face
Wellnigh was hidden in the minster gloom;
But there was heard among the holy hymns
A voice as of the waters, for she dwells
Down in a deep, calm, whatsoever storms
May shake the world, and when the surface rolls,
Hath power to walk the waters like our Lord.

"There likewise I beheld Excalibur
Before him at his crowning borne, the sword
That rose from out the bosom of the lake,
And Arthur row'd across and took it—rich
With jewels, elfin Urim, on the hilt,
Bewildering heart and eye—the blade so bright
That men are blinded by it—on one side,
Graven in the oldest tongue of all this world,
'Take me,' but turn the blade and you shall see,

And written in the speech ye speak yourself,
'Cast me away!' And sad was Arthur's face
Taking it, but old Merlin counsell'd him,
'Take thou and strike! the time to cast away
Is yet far-off.' So this great brand the king
Took, and by this will beat his foemen down."

Thereat Leodogran rejoiced, but thought
To sift his doubtings to the last, and ask'd,
Fixing full eyes of question on her face,
"The swallow and the swift are near akin,
But thou art closer to this noble prince,
Being his own dear sister;" and she said,
"Daughter of Gorloïs and Ygerne am I;"
"And therefore Arthur's sister," ask'd the King.
She answer'd, "These be secret things," and sign'd
To those two sons to pass and let them be.
And Gawain went, and breaking into song

Sprang out, and follow'd by his flying hair
Ran like a colt, and leapt at all he saw:
But Modred laid his ear beside the doors,
And there half heard; the same that afterward
Struck for the throne, and striking found his doom.

And then the Queen made answer, "What know I?
For dark my mother was in eyes and hair,
And dark in hair and eyes am I; and dark
Was Gorloïs, yea and dark was Uther too,
Wellnigh to blackness; but this king is fair
Beyond the race of Britons and of men.
Moreover always in my mind I hear
A cry from out the dawning of my life,
A mother weeping, and I hear her say,
'O that ye had some brother, pretty one,
To guard thee on the rough ways of the world.'"

"Ay," said the King, "and hear ye such a cry?
But when did Arthur chance upon thee first?"

"O king!" she cried, "and I will tell thee true:
He found me first when yet a little maid:
Beaten I had been for a little fault
Whereof I was not guilty; and out I ran
And flung myself down on a bank of heath,
And hated this fair world and all therein,
And wept, and wish'd that I were dead; and he—
I know not whether of himself he came,
Or brought by Merlin, who, they say, can walk
Unseen at pleasure—he was at my side,
And spake sweet words, and comforted my heart,
And dried my tears, being a child with me.
And many a time he came, and evermore
As I grew greater grew with me; and sad
At times he seem'd, and sad with him was I,

Stern too at times, and then I loved him not,
But sweet again, and then I loved him well.
And now of late I see him less and less,
But those first days had golden hours for me,
For then I surely thought he would be king.

"But let me tell thee now another tale:
For Bleys, our Merlin's master, as they say,
Died but of late, and sent his cry to me,
To hear him speak before he left his life.
Shrunk like a fairy changeling lay the mage,
And when I enter'd told me that himself
And Merlin ever served about the king,
Uther, before he died, and on the night
When Uther in Tintagil past away
Moaning and wailing for an heir, the two
Left the still king, and passing forth to breathe,
Then from the castle gateway by the chasm

Descending thro' the dismal night—a night
In which the bounds of heaven and earth were lost—
Beheld, so high upon the dreary deeps
It seem'd in heaven, a ship, the shape thereof
A dragon wing'd, and all from stem to stern
Bright with a shining people on the decks,
And gone as soon as seen. And then the two
Dropt to the cove, and watch'd the great sea fall,
Wave after wave, each mightier than the last,
Till last, a ninth one, gathering half the deep
And full of voices, slowly rose and plunged
Roaring, and all the wave was in a flame:
And down the wave and in the flame was borne
A naked babe, and rode to Merlin's feet,
Who stoopt and caught the babe, and cried 'The
    King!
Here is an heir for Uther!' And the fringe
Of that great breaker, sweeping up the strand,

Lash'd at the wizard as he spake the word,
And all at once all round him rose in fire,
So that the child and he were clothed in fire.
And presently thereafter follow'd calm,
Free sky and stars: 'And this same child,' he said,
'Is he who reigns; nor could I part in peace
Till this were told.' And saying this the seer
Went thro' the strait and dreadful pass of death,
Not ever to be question'd any more
Save on the further side; but when I met
Merlin, and ask'd him if these things were truth—
The shining dragon and the naked child
Descending in the glory of the seas—
He laugh'd as is his wont, and answer'd me
In riddling triplets of old time, and said:

"'Rain, rain, and sun! a rainbow in the sky!
A young man will be wiser by and by;

An old man's wit may wander ere he die.

Rain, rain, and sun! a rainbow on the lea!
And truth is this to me, and that to thee;
And truth or clothed or naked let it be.
Rain, sun, and rain! and the free blossom blows:
Sun, rain, and sun! and where is he who knows?
From the great deep to the great deep he goes.'

"So Merlin riddling anger'd me; but thou
Fear not to give this king thine only child,
Guinevere: so great bards of him will sing
Hereafter; and dark sayings from of old
Ranging and ringing thro' the minds of men,
And echo'd by old folk beside their fires
For comfort after their wage-work is done,
Speak of the king; and Merlin in our time
Hath spoken also, not in jest, and sworn
Tho' men may wound him that he will not die,

But pass, again to come; and then or now
Utterly smite the heathen underfoot,
Till these and all men hail him for their king."

She spake and King Leodogran rejoiced,
But musing "Shall I answer yea or nay?"
Doubted, and drowsed, nodded and slept, and saw,
Dreaming, a slope of land that ever grew,
Field after field, up to a height, the peak
Haze-hidden, and thereon a phantom king,
Now looming, and now lost; and on the slope
The sword rose, the hind fell, the herd was driven,
Fire glimpsed; and all the land from roof and rick,
In drifts of smoke before a rolling wind,
Stream'd to the peak, and mingled with the haze
And made it thicker; while the phantom king
Sent out at times a voice; and here or there

Stood one who pointed toward the voice, the rest
Slew on and burnt, crying, "No king of ours,
No son of Uther, and no king of ours;"
Till with a wink his dream was changed, the haze
Descended, and the solid earth became
As nothing, and the king stood out in heaven,
Crown'd. And Leodogran awoke, and sent
Ulfius, and Brastias and Bedivere,
Back to the court of Arthur answering yea.

Then Arthur charged his warrior whom he loved
And honour'd most, Sir Lancelot, to ride forth
And bring the Queen;—and watch'd him from the
    gates;
And Lancelot past away among the flowers,
(For then was latter April) and return'd
Among the flowers, in May, with Guinevere.
To whom arrived, by Dubric the high saint,

Chief of the church in Britain, and before
The stateliest of her altar-shrines, the king
That morn was married, while in stainless white,
The fair beginners of a nobler time,
And glorying in their vows and him, his knights
Stood round him, and rejoicing in his joy.
And holy Dubric spread his hands and spake,
"Reign ye, and live and love, and make the world
Other, and may thy Queen be one with thee,
And all this Order of the Table Round
Fulfil the boundless purpose of their king."

Then at the marriage feast came in from Rome,
The slowly-fading mistress of the world,
Great lords, who claim'd the tribute as of yore.
But Arthur spake, "Behold, for these have sworn
To fight my wars, and worship me their king;
The old order changeth, yielding place to new;

And we that fight for our fair father Christ,
Seeing that ye be grown too weak and old
To drive the heathen from your Roman wall,
No tribute will we pay:" so those great lords
Drew back in wrath, and Arthur strove with Rome.

And Arthur and his knighthood for a space
Were all one will, and thro' that strength the king
Drew in the petty princedoms under him,
Fought, and in twelve great battles overcame
The heathen hordes, and made a realm and reign'd.

THE HOLY GRAIL.

THE HOLY GRAIL.

FROM noiseful arms, and acts of prowess done
In tournament or tilt, Sir Percivale,
Whom Arthur and his knighthood call'd The Pure,
Had pass'd into the silent life of prayer,
Praise, fast, and alms; and leaving for the cowl
The helmet in an abbey far away
From Camelot, there, and not long after, died.

And one, a fellow-monk among the rest,
Ambrosius, loved him much beyond the rest,
And honour'd him, and wrought into his heart

A way by love that waken'd love within,
To answer that which came: and as they sat
Beneath a world-old yew-tree, darkening half
The cloisters, on a gustful April morn
That puff'd the swaying branches into smoke
Above them, ere the summer when he died,
The monk Ambrosius question'd Percivale:

"O brother, I have seen this yew-tree smoke,
Spring after spring, for half a hundred years:
For never have I known the world without,
Nor ever stray'd beyond the pale: but thee,
When first thou camest—such a courtesy
Spake thro' the limbs and in the voice—I knew
For one of those who eat in Arthur's hall;
For good ye are and bad, and like to coins,
Some true, some light, but every one of you
Stamp'd with the image of the King; and now

Tell me, what drove thee from the Table Round,
My brother? was it earthly passion crost?"

"Nay," said the knight; "for no such passion mine.
But the sweet vision of the Holy Grail
Drove me from all vainglories, rivalries,
And earthly heats that spring and sparkle out
Among us in the jousts, while women watch
Who wins, who falls; and waste the spiritual strength
Within us, better offer'd up to Heaven."

To whom the monk: "The Holy Grail!—I trust
We are green in Heaven's eyes; but here too much
We moulder—as to things without I mean—
Yet one of your own knights, a guest of ours,
Told us of this in our refectory,

But spake with such a sadness and so low
We heard not half of what he said. What is it?
The phantom of a cup that comes and goes?"

"Nay, monk! what phantom?" answer'd Percivale.
"The cup, the cup itself, from which our Lord
Drank at the last sad supper with his own.
This, from the blessed land of Aromat—
After the day of darkness, when the dead
Went wandering o'er Moriah—the good saint,
Arimathæan Joseph, journeying brought
To Glastonbury, where the winter thorn
Blossoms at Christmas, mindful of our Lord.
And there awhile it bode; and if a man
Could touch or see it, he was heal'd at once,
By faith, of all his ills. But then the times
Grew to such evil that the holy cup
Was caught away to Heaven, and disappear'd."

To whom the monk: "From our old books I know
That Joseph came of old to Glastonbury,
And there the heathen Prince, Arviragus,
Gave him an isle of marsh whereon to build;
And there he built with wattles from the marsh
A little lonely church in days of yore,
For so they say, these books of ours, but seem
Mute of this miracle, for as I have read.
But who first saw the holy thing to-day?"

"A woman," answer'd Percivale, "a nun,
And one no further off in blood from me
Than sister; and if ever holy maid
With knees of adoration wore the stone,
A holy maid; tho' never maiden glow'd,
But that was in her earlier maidenhood,
With such a fervent flame of human love,
Which being rudely blunted, glanced and shot

Only to holy things; to prayer and praise
She gave herself, to fast and alms. And yet,
Nun as she was, the scandal of the Court,
Sin against Arthur and the Table Round,
And the strange sound of an adulterous race,
Across the iron grating of her cell
Beat, and she pray'd and fasted all the more.

"And he to whom she told her sins, or what
Her all but utter whiteness held for sin,
A man well-nigh a hundred winters old,
Spake often with her of the Holy Grail,
A legend handed down thro' five or six,
And each of these a hundred winters old,
From our Lord's time. And when King Arthur made
His Table Round, and all men's hearts became
Clean for a season, surely he had thought
That now the Holy Grail would come again;

But sin broke out. Ah, Christ, that it would come,
And heal the world of all their wickedness!
'O Father!' asked the maiden, 'might it come
To me by prayer and fasting?' 'Nay,' said he,
'I know not, for thy heart is pure as snow.'
And so she pray'd and fasted, till the sun
Shone, and the wind blew, thro' her, and I thought
She might have risen and floated when I saw her.

"For on a day she sent to speak with me.
And when she came to speak, behold her eyes
Beyond my knowing of them, beautiful,
Beyond all knowing of them, wonderful,
Beautiful in the light of holiness.
And 'O my brother, Percivale,' she said,
'Sweet brother, I have seen the Holy Grail:
For, waked at dead of night, I heard a sound
As of a silver horn from o'er the hills

Blown, and I thought, "It is not Arthur's use
To hunt by moonlight;" and the slender sound
As from a distance beyond distance grew
Coming upon me—O never harp nor horn,
Nor aught we blow with breath, or touch with
      hand,
Was like that music as it came; and then
Stream'd thro' my cell a cold and silver beam,
And down the long beam stole the Holy Grail,
Rose-red with beatings in it, as if alive,
Till all the white walls of my cell were dyed
With rosy colours leaping on the wall;
And then the music faded, and the Grail
Pass'd, and the beam decay'd, and from the walls
The rosy quiverings died into the night.
So now the Holy Thing is here again
Among us, brother, fast thou too and pray,
And tell thy brother knights to fast and pray,

That so perchance the vision may be seen
By thee and those, and all the world be heal'd.'

"Then leaving the pale nun, I spake of this
To all men; and myself fasted and pray'd
Always, and many among us many a week
Fasted and pray'd even to the uttermost,
Expectant of the wonder that would be.

"And one there was among us, ever moved
Among us in white armour, Galahad.
'God make thee good as thou art beautiful,'
Said Arthur, when he dubb'd him knight; and none,
In so young youth, was ever made a knight
Till Galahad; and this Galahad, when he heard
My sister's vision, fill'd me with amaze;
His eyes became so like her own, they seem'd
Hers, and himself her brother more than I.

"Sister or brother none had he; but some
Call'd him a son of Lancelot, and some said
Begotten by enchantment—chatterers they,
Like birds of passage piping up and down,
That gape for flies—we know not whence they come;
For when was Lancelot wanderingly lewd?

"But she, the wan sweet maiden shore away
Clean from her forehead all that wealth of hair
Which made a silken mat-work for her feet;
And out of this she plaited broad and long
A strong sword-belt, and wove with silver thread
And crimson in the belt a strange device,
A crimson grail within a silver beam;
And saw the bright boy-knight, and bound it on him,
Saying, 'My knight, my love, my knight of heaven,
O thou, my love, whose love is one with mine,
I, maiden, round thee, maiden, bind my belt.

Go forth, for thou shalt see what I have seen,
And break thro' all, till one will crown thee king
Far in the spiritual city:' and as she spake
She sent the deathless passion in her eyes
Thro' him, and made him hers, and laid her mind
On him, and he believed in her belief.

"Then came a year of miracle: O brother,
In our great hall there stood a vacant chair,
Fashion'd by Merlin ere he past away,
And carven with strange figures; and in and out
The figures, like a serpent, ran a scroll
Of letters in a tongue no man could read.
And Merlin call'd it 'The Siege perilous,'
Perilous for good and ill; 'for there,' he said,
'No man could sit but he should lose himself:'
And once by misadvertence Merlin sat
In his own chair, and so was lost; but he,

Galahad, when he heard of Merlin's doom,
Cried, 'If I lose myself I save myself!'

"Then on a summer night it came to pass,
While the great banquet lay along the hall,
That Galahad would sit down in Merlin's chair.

"And all at once, as there we sat, we heard
A cracking and a riving of the roofs,
And rending, and a blast, and overhead
Thunder, and in the thunder was a cry.
And in the blast there smote along the hall
A beam of light seven times more clear than day;
And down the long beam stole the Holy Grail
All over cover'd with a luminous cloud,
And none might see who bare it, and it past.
But every knight beheld his fellow's face
As in a glory, and all the knights arose,

And staring each at other like dumb men
Stood, till I found a voice and sware a vow.

"I sware a vow before them all, that I,
Because I had not seen the Grail, would ride
A twelvemonth and a day in quest of it,
Until I found and saw it, as the nun
My sister saw it; and Galahad sware the vow,
And good Sir Bors, our Lancelot's cousin, sware,
And Lancelot sware, and many among the knights,
And Gawain sware, and louder than the rest."

Then spake the monk Ambrosius, asking him,
"What said the King? Did Arthur take the vow?"

"Nay, for my lord," said Percivale, "the King,
Was not in hall: for early that same day,
Scaped thro' a cavern from a bandit hold,

An outraged maiden sprang into the hall
Crying on help: for all her shining hair
Was smear'd with earth, and either milky arm
Red-rent with hooks of bramble, and all she
        wore
Torn as a sail that leaves the rope is torn
In tempest: so the King arose and went
To smoke the scandalous hive of those wild bees
That made such honey in his realm. Howbeit
Some little of this marvel he too saw,
Returning o'er the plain that then began
To darken under Camelot; whence the King
Look'd up, calling aloud, 'Lo there! the roofs
Of our great hall are rolled in thunder-smoke!
Pray Heaven, they be not smitten by the bolt.'
For dear to Arthur was that hall of ours,
As having there so oft with all his knights
Feasted, and as the stateliest under heaven.

"O brother, had you known our mighty hall,
Which Merlin built for Arthur long ago!
For all the sacred mount of Camelot,
And all the dim rich city, roof by roof,
Tower after tower, spire beyond spire,
By grove, and garden-lawn, and rushing brook,
Climbs to the mighty hall that Merlin built.
And four great zones of sculpture, set betwixt
With many a mystic symbol, gird the hall:
And in the lowest beasts are slaying men,
And in the second men are slaying beasts,
And on the third are warriors, perfect men,
And on the fourth are men with growing wings,
And over all one statue in the mould
Of Arthur, made by Merlin, with a crown,
And peak'd wings pointed to the Northern Star.
And eastward fronts the statue, and the crown
And both the wings are made of gold, and flame

At sunrise till the people in far fields,
Wasted so often by the heathen hordes,
Behold it, crying, 'We have still a king.'

"And, brother, had you known our hall within,
Broader and higher than any in all the lands!
Where twelve great windows blazon Arthur's wars,
And all the light that falls upon the board
Streams thro' the twelve great battles of our
        King.
Nay, one there is, and at the eastern end,
Wealthy with wandering lines of mount and mere,
Where Arthur finds the brand, Excalibur.
And also one to the west, and counter to it,
And blank: and who shall blazon it? when and
        how?—
O there, perchance, when all our wars are done,
The brand Excalibur will be cast away.

"So to this hall full quickly rode the King,
In horror lest the work by Merlin wrought,
Dreamlike, should on the sudden vanish, wrapt
In unremorseful folds of rolling fire.
And in he rode, and up I glanced, and saw
The golden dragon sparkling over all:
And many of those who burnt the hold, their arms
Hack'd, and their foreheads grimed with smoke, and sear'd,
Follow'd, and in among bright faces, ours,
Full of the vision, prest· and then the King
Spake to me, being nearest, 'Percivale,'
(Because the hall was all in tumult—some
Vowing, and some protesting), 'what is this?'

"O brother, when I told him what had chanced,
My sister's vision, and the rest, his face
Darken'd, as I have seen it more than once,

When some brave deed seem'd to be done in vain,
Darken; and 'Woe is me, my knights,' he cried,
'Had I been here, ye had not sworn the vow.'
Bold was mine answer, 'Had thyself been here,
My King, thou wouldst have sworn.' 'Yea, yea,'
  said he,
'Art thou so bold and hast not seen the Grail?'

"'Nay, Lord, I heard the sound, I saw the light,
But since I did not see the Holy Thing,
I sware a vow to follow it till I saw.'

"Then when he asked us, knight by knight, if any
Had seen it, all their answers were as one:
'Nay, Lord, and therefore have we sworn our vows'.

"'Lo now,' said Arthur, 'have ye seen a cloud?
What go ye into the wilderness to see?'

Then Galahad on the sudden, and in a voice
Shrilling along the hall to Arthur, call'd,
'But I, Sir Arthur, saw the Holy Grail,
I saw the Holy Grail and heard a cry—
"O Galahad, and O Galahad, follow me."

"'Ah, Galahad, Galahad,' said the King, 'for such
As thou art is the vision, not for these.
Thy holy nun and thou have seen a sign—
Holier is none, my Percivale, than she—
A sign to maim this Order which I made.
But you, that follow but the leader's bell'
(Brother, the King was hard upon his knights)
'Taliessin is our fullest throat of song,
And one hath sung and all the dumb will sing.
Lancelot is Lancelot, and hath overborne
Five knights at once, and every younger knight,
Unproven, holds himself as Lancelot,

Till overborne by one, he learns—and ye,
What are ye? Galahads?—no, nor Percivales'
(For thus it pleased the King to range me close
After Sir Galahad); 'nay,' said he, 'but men
With strength and will to right the wrong'd, of power
To lay the sudden heads of violence flat,
Knights that in twelve great battles splash'd and dyed
The strong White Horse in his own heathen blood—
But one hath seen, and all the blind will see.
Go, since your vows are sacred, being made:
Yet—for ye know the cries of all my realm
Pass thro' this hall—how often, O my knights,
Your places being vacant at my side,
This chance of noble deeds will come and go
Unchallenged, while you follow wandering fires
Lost in the quagmire? Many of you, yea most,
Return no more: ye think I show myself
Too dark a prophet: come now, let us meet

The morrow morn once more in one full field
Of gracious pastime, that once more the King,
Before you leave him for this Quest, may count
The yet-unbroken strength of all his knights,
Rejoicing in that Order which he made.'

"So when the sun broke next from under ground,
All the great table of our Arthur closed
And clash'd in such a tourney and so full,
So many lances broken—never yet
Had Camelot seen the like, since Arthur came;
And I myself and Galahad, for a strength
Was in us from the vision, overthrew
So many knights that all the people cried,
And almost burst the barriers in their heat,
Shouting 'Sir Galahad and Sir Percivale!'

"But when the next day brake from under ground—

O brother, had you known our Camelot,
Built by old Kings, age after age, so old
The King himself had fears that it would fall,
So strange, and rich, and dim; for where the roofs
Totter'd toward each other in the sky,
Met foreheads all along the street of those
Who watch'd us pass; and lower, and where the long
Rich galleries, lady-laden, weigh'd the necks
Of dragons clinging to the crazy walls,
Thicker than drops from thunder, showers of flowers
Fell as we past; and men and boys astride
On wyvern, lion, dragon, griffin, swan,
At all the corners, named us each by name,
Calling 'God speed!' but in the street below
The knights and ladies wept, and rich and poor
Wept, and the King himself could hardly speak
For grief, and in the middle street the Queen,
Who rode by Lancelot, wail'd and shriek'd aloud,

'This madness has come on us for our sins.'
And then we reach'd the weirdly-sculptured gate,
Where Arthur's wars were render'd mystically,
And thence departed every one his way.

"And I was lifted up in heart, and thought
Of all my late-shown prowess in the lists,
How my strong lance had beaten down the knights,
So many and famous names; and never yet
Had heaven appear'd so blue, nor earth so green,
For all my blood danced in me, and I knew
That I should light upon the Holy Grail.

"Thereafter, the dark warning of our King,
That most of us would follow wandering fires,
Came like a driving gloom across my mind.
Then every evil word I had spoken once,
And every evil thought I had thought of old,

And every evil deed I ever did,
Awoke and cried, 'This Quest is not for thee.'
And lifting up mine eyes, I found myself
Alone, and in a land of sand and thorns,
And I was thirsty even unto death;
And I, too, cried, 'This Quest is not for thee.'

"And on I rode, and when I thought my thirst
Would slay me, saw deep lawns, and then a brook,
With one sharp rapid, where the crisping white
Play'd ever back upon the sloping wave,
And took both ear and eye; and o'er the brook
Were apple-trees, and apples by the brook
Fallen, and on the lawns. 'I will rest here,'
I said, 'I am not worthy of the Quest;'
But even while I drank the brook, and ate
The goodly apples, all these things at once
Fell into dust, and I was left alone,

And thirsting, in a land of sand and thorns.

"And then behold a woman at a door
Spinning; and fair the house whereby she sat,
And kind the woman's eyes and innocent,
And all her bearing gracious; and she rose
Opening her arms to meet me, as who should say,
'Rest here;' but when I touched her, lo! she, too,
Fell into dust and nothing, and the house
Became no better than a broken shed,
And in it a dead babe; and also this
Fell into dust, and I was left alone.

"And on I rode, and greater was my thirst.
Then flash'd a yellow gleam across the world,
And where it smote the plowshare in the field,
The plowman left his plowing, and fell down
Before it; where it glitter'd on her pail,

The milkmaid left her milking, and fell down
Before it, and I knew not why, but thought
'The sun is rising,' tho' the sun had risen.
Then was I ware of one that on me moved
In golden armour with a crown of gold
About a casque all jewels; and his horse
In golden armour jewell'd everywhere:
And on the splendour came, flashing me blind;
And seem'd to me the Lord of all the world,
Being so huge. But when I thought he meant
To crush me, moving on me, lo! he, too,
Opened his arms to embrace me as he came,
And up I went and touch'd him, and he, too,
Fell into dust, and I was left alone
And wearying in a land of sand and thorns.

"And I rode on and found a mighty hill,
And on the top, a city wall'd: the spires

Prick'd with incredible pinnacles into heaven.
And by the gateway stirr'd a crowd; and these
Cried to me climbing, 'Welcome, Percivale!
Thou mightiest and thou purest among men!'
And glad was I and clomb, but found at top
No man, nor any voice. And thence I past
Far thro' a ruinous city, and I saw
That man had once dwelt there; but there I found
Only one man of an exceeding age.
'Where is that goodly company,' said I,
'That so cried out upon me?' and he had
Scarce any voice to answer, and yet gasp'd
'Whence and what art thou?' and even as he
      spoke
Fell into dust, and disappear'd, and I
Was left alone once more, and cried in grief,
'Lo, if I find the Holy Grail itself
And touch it, it will crumble into dust.'

"And thence I dropt into a lowly vale,
Low as the hill was high, and where the vale
Was lowest, found a chapel and thereby
A holy hermit in a hermitage,
To whom I told my phantoms, and he said:

"'O son, thou hast not true humility,
The highest virtue, mother of them all;
For when the Lord of all things made Himself
Naked of glory for His mortal change,
"Take thou my robe," she said, "for all is thine,"
And all her form shone forth with sudden light
So that the angels were amazed, and she
Follow'd him down, and like a flying star
Led on the gray-hair'd wisdom of the east;
But her thou hast not known: for what is this
Thou thoughtest of thy prowess and thy sins?
Thou hast not lost thyself to save thyself

As Galahad.' When the hermit made an end,
In silver armour suddenly Galahad shone
Before us, and against the chapel door
Laid lance, and enter'd, and we knelt in prayer.
And there the hermit slaked my burning thirst
And at the sacring of the mass I saw
The holy elements alone; but he:
'Saw ye no more? I, Galahad, saw the Grail,
The Holy Grail, descend upon the shrine:
I saw the fiery face as of a child
That smote itself into the bread, and went;
And hither am I come; and never yet
Hath what thy sister taught me first to see,
This Holy Thing, fail'd from my side, nor come
Cover'd, but moving with me night and day,
Fainter by day, but always in the night
Blood-red, and sliding down the blacken'd marsh
Blood-red, and on the naked mountain top

Blood-red, and in the sleeping mere below
Blood-red. And in the strength of this I rode,
Shattering all evil customs everywhere,
And past thro' Pagan realms, and made them mine,
And clash'd with Pagan hordes, and bore them down,
And broke thro' all, and in the strength of this
Come victor. But my time is hard at hand,
And hence I go; and one will crown me king
Far in the spiritual city; and come thou, too,
For thou shalt see the vision when I go.'

"While thus he spake, his eye, dwelling on mine,
Drew me, with power upon me, till I grew
One with him, to believe as he believed.
Then, when the day began to wane, we went.

"There rose a hill that none but man could climb,
Scarr'd with a hundred wintry watercourses—

Storm at the top, and when we gain'd it, storm
Round us and death; for every moment glanced
His silver arms and gloom'd: so quick and thick
The lightnings here and there to left and right
Struck, till the dry old trunks about us, dead,
Yea, rotten with a hundred years of death,
Sprang into fire: and at the base we found
On either hand, as far as eye could see,
A great black swamp and of an evil smell,
Part black, part whiten'd with the bones of men,
Not to be crost, save that some ancient king
Had built a way, where, link'd with many a bridge,
A thousand piers ran into the great Sea.
And Galahad fled along them bridge by bridge,
And every bridge as quickly as he crost
Sprang into fire and vanish'd, tho' I yearn'd
To follow; and thrice above him all the heavens
Open'd and blazed with thunder such as seem'd

Shoutings of all the sons of God: and first
At once I saw him far on the great Sea,
In silver-shining armour starry-clear;
And o'er his head the holy vessel hung
Clothed in white samite or a luminous cloud.
And with exceeding swiftness ran the boat
If boat it were—I saw not whence it came.
And when the heavens open'd and blazed again
Roaring, I saw him like a silver star—
And had he set the sail, or had the boat
Become a living creature clad with wings?
And o'er his head the holy vessel hung
Redder than any rose, a joy to me,
For now I knew the veil had been withdrawn.
Then in a moment when they blazed again
Opening, I saw the least of little stars
Down on the waste, and straight beyond the star
I saw the spiritual city and all her spires

And gateways in a glory like one pearl—
No larger, tho' the goal of all the saints—
Strike from the sea; and from the star there shot
A rose-red sparkle to the city, and there
Dwelt, and I knew it was the Holy Grail,
Which never eyes on earth again shall see.
Then fell the floods of heaven drowning the deep.
And how my feet recross'd the deathful ridge
No memory in me lives; but that I touch'd
The chapel-doors at dawn I know; and thence
Taking my war-horse from the holy man,
Glad that no phantom vext me more, return'd
To whence I came, the gate of Arthur's wars."

"O brother," ask'd Ambrosius,—"for in sooth
These ancient books—and they would win thee—teem,
Only I find not there this Holy Grail,
With miracles and marvels like to these,

66 THE HOLY GRAIL

Not all unlike; which oftentime I read,
Who read but on my breviary with ease,
Till my head swims; and then go forth and pass
Down to the little thorpe that lies so close,
And almost plaster'd like a martin's nest
To these old walls—and mingle with our folk;
And knowing every honest face of theirs,
As well as ever shepherd knew his sheep,
And every homely secret in their hearts,
Delight myself with gossip and old wives,
And ills and aches, and teethings, lyings-in,
And mirthful sayings, children of the place,
That have no meaning half a league away:
Or lulling random squabbles when they rise,
Chafferings and chatterings at the market-cross,
Rejoice, small man, in this small world of mine,
Yea, even in their hens and in their eggs—
O brother, saving this Sir Galahad

Came ye on none but phantoms in your quest,
No man, no woman?"

      Then, Sir Percivale:
"All men, to one so bound by such a vow,
And women were as phantoms. O, my brother,
Why wilt thou shame me to confess to thee
How far I falter'd from my quest and vow?
For after I had lain so many nights
A bedmate of the snail and eft and snake,
In grass and burdock, I was changed to wan
And meagre, and the vision had not come,
And then I chanced upon a goodly town
With one great dwelling in the middle of it;
Thither I made, and there was I disarm'd
By maidens each as fair as any flower:
But when they led me into hall, behold
The Princess of that castle was the one,

Brother, and that one only, who had ever
Made my heart leap; for when I moved of old
A slender page about her father's hall,
And she a slender maiden, all my heart
Went after her with longing: yet we twain
Had never kiss'd a kiss, or vow'd a vow.
And now I came upon her once again,
And one had wedded her, and he was dead,
And all his land and wealth and state were hers.
And while I tarried, every day she set
A banquet richer than the day before
By me; for all her longing and her will
Was toward me as of old; till one fair morn,
I walking to and fro beside a stream
That flash'd across her orchard underneath
Her castle-walls, she stole upon my walk,
And calling me the greatest of all knights,
Embraced me, and so kiss'd me the first time,

And gave herself and all her wealth to me.
Then I remember'd Arthur's warning word,
That most of us would follow wandering fires,
And the Quest faded in my heart. Anon,
The heads of all her people drew to me,
With supplication both of knees and tongue:
'We have heard of thee: thou art our greatest knight,
Our Lady says it, and we well believe:
Wed thou our Lady, and rule over us,
And thou shalt be as Arthur in our land.'
O me, my brother! but one night my vow
Burnt me within, so that I rose and fled,
But wail'd and wept, and hated mine own self,
And ev'n the Holy Quest, and all but her;
Then after I was join'd with Galahad
Cared not for her, nor anything upon earth."

Then said the monk, "Poor men, when yule is cold,

Must be content to sit by little fires.
And this am I, so that ye care for me
Ever so little; yea, and blest be Heaven
That brought thee here to this poor house of ours,
Where all the brethren are so hard, to warm
My cold heart with a friend: but O the pity
To find thine own first love once more—to hold,
Hold her a wealthy bride within thine arms,
Or all but hold, and then—cast her aside,
Foregoing all her sweetness, like a weed.
For we that want the warmth of double life,
We that are plagued with dreams of something
    sweet
Beyond all sweetness in a life so rich,—
Ah, blessed Lord, I speak too earthlywise,
Seeing I never stray'd beyond the cell,
But live like an old badger in his earth,
With earth about him everywhere, despite

All fast and penance. Saw ye none beside,
None of your knights?"

                "Yea so," said Percivale:
"One night my pathway swerving east, I saw
The pelican on the casque of our Sir Bors
All in the middle of the rising moon:
And toward him spurr'd and hail'd him, and he me,
And each made joy of either; then he ask'd,
'Where is he? hast thou seen him—Lancelot?'
        'Once,'
Said good Sir Bors, 'he dash'd across me—mad,
And maddening what he rode: and when I cried,
"Ridest thou then so hotly on a quest
So holy?" Lancelot shouted, "Stay me not!
I have been the sluggard, and I ride apace,
For now there is a lion in the way."
So vanish'd.'

"Then Sir Bors had ridden on
Softly, and sorrowing for our Lancelot,
Because his former madness, once the talk
And scandal of our table, had return'd;
For Lancelot's kith and kin so worship him
That ill to him is ill to them; to Bors
Beyond the rest: he well had been content
Not to have seen, so Lancelot might have seen,
The Holy Cup of healing; and, indeed,
Being so clouded with his grief and love,
Small heart was his after the Holy Quest:
If God would send the vision, well: if not,
The Quest and he were in the hands of heaven.

"And then, with small adventure met, Sir Bors
Rode to the lonest tract of all the realm,
And found a people there among their crags,
Our race and blood, a remnant that were left

Paynim amid their circles, and the stones
They pitch up straight to heaven: and their wise
    men
Were strong in that old magic which can trace
The wandering of the stars, and scoff'd at him
And this high Quest as at a simple thing:
Told him he follow'd—almost Arthur's words—
A mocking fire: 'what other fire than he,
Whereby the blood beats, and the blossom blows,
And the sea rolls, and all the world is warm'd?'
And when his answer chafed them, the rough crowd,
Hearing he had a difference with their priests,
Seized him, and bound and plunged him into a cell
Of great piled stones; and lying bounden there
In darkness thro' innumerable hours
He heard the hollow-ringing heavens sweep
Over him, till by miracle—what else?—
Heavy as it was, a great stone slipt and fell,

Such as no wind could move: and thro' the gap
Glimmer'd the streaming scud; then came a night
Still as the day was loud; and thro' the gap
The seven clear stars of Arthur's Table Round—
For, brother, so one night, because they roll
Thro' such a round in heaven, we named the stars,
Rejoicing in ourselves and in our king—
And these, like bright eyes of familiar friends,
In on him shone, 'And then to me, to me,'
Said good Sir Bors, 'beyond all hopes of mine,
Who scarce had pray'd or ask'd it for myself—
Across the seven clear stars—O grace to me—
In colour like the fingers of a hand
Before a burning taper, the sweet Grail
Glided and past, and close upon it peal'd
A sharp quick thunder.' Afterwards a maid,
Who kept our holy faith among her kin
In secret, entering, loosed and let him go."

To whom the monk: "And I remember now
That pelican on the casque: Sir Bors it was
Who spake so low and sadly at our board;
And mighty reverent at our grace was he:
A square-set man and honest; and his eyes,
An out-door sign of all the warmth within,
Smiled with his lips—a smile beneath a cloud,
But heaven had meant it for a sunny one:
Ay, ay, Sir Bors, who else? But when ye reach'd
The city, found ye all your knights return'd,
Or was there sooth in Arthur's prophecy,
Tell me, and what said each, and what the King?"

Then answer'd Percivale: "And that can I,
Brother, and truly; since the living words
Of so great men as Lancelot and our King
Pass not from door to door and out again,
But sit within the house. O, when we reach'd

The city, our horses stumbling as they trode
On heaps of ruin, hornless unicorns,
Crack'd basilisks, and splinter'd cockatrices,
And shatter'd talbots, which had left the stones
Raw, that they fell from, brought us to the hall.

"And there sat Arthur on the daïs-throne,
And those that had gone out upon the Quest,
Wasted and worn, and but a tithe of them,
And those that had not, stood before the King.
Who, when he saw me, rose, and bade me hail,
Saying, 'A welfare in thine eye reproves
Our fear of some disastrous chance for thee
On hill, or plain, at sea, or flooding ford.
So fierce a gale made havock here of late
Among the strange devices of our kings;
Yea, shook this newer, stronger hall of ours,
And from the statue Merlin moulded for us

Half-wrench'd a golden wing; but now—the quest,
This vision—hast thou seen the Holy Cup,
That Joseph brought of old to Glastonbury?'

"So when I told him all thyself hast heard,
Ambrosius, and my fresh but fixt resolve
To pass away into the quiet life,
He answer'd not, but, sharply turning, ask'd
Of Gawain, 'Gawain, was this Quest for thee?'

"'Nay, lord,' said Gawain, 'not for such as I.
Therefore I communed with a saintly man,
Who made me sure the Quest was not for me;
For I was much awearied of the Quest:
But found a silk pavilion in a field,
And merry maidens in it; and then this gale
Tore my pavilion from the tenting-pin,
And blew my merry maidens all about

With all discomfort; yea, and but for this,
My twelvemonth and a day were pleasant to me.'

"He ceased; and Arthur turn'd to whom at first
He saw not, for Sir Bors, on entering, push'd
Athwart the throng to Lancelot, caught his hand,
Held it, and there, half-hidden by him, stood,
Until the King espied him, saying to him,
'Hail, Bors! if ever loyal man and true
Could see it, thou hast seen the Grail;' and Bors,
'Ask me not, for I may not speak of it,
I saw it:' and the tears were in his eyes.

"Then there remain'd but Lancelot, for the rest
Spake but of sundry perils in the storm;
Perhaps, like him of Cana in Holy Writ,
Our Arthur kept his best until the last;

'Thou, too, my Lancelot,' ask'd the King, 'my
    friend,
Our mightiest, hath this Quest avail'd for thee?'

"'Our mightiest!' answer'd Lancelot, with a groan;
'O King!'—and when he paused, methought I spied
A dying fire of madness in his eyes—
'O King, my friend, if friend of thine I be,
Happier are those that welter in their sin,
Swine in the mud, that cannot see for slime,
Slime of the ditch: but in me lived a sin
So strange, of such a kind, that all of pure,
Noble, and knightly in me twined and clung
Round that one sin, until the wholesome flower
And poisonous grew together, each as each,
Not to be pluck'd asunder; and when thy knights
Sware, I sware with them only in the hope
That could I touch or see the Holy Grail

They might be pluck'd asunder. Then I spake
To one most holy saint, who wept and said,
That save they could be pluck'd asunder, all
My quest were but in vain; to whom I vow'd
That I would work according as he will'd.
And forth I went, and while I yearn'd and strove
To tear the twain asunder in my heart,
My madness came upon me as of old,
And whipt me into waste fields far away;
There was I beaten down by little men,
Mean knights, to whom the moving of my sword
And shadow of my spear had been enow
To scare them from me once; and then I came
All in my folly to the naked shore,
Wide flats, where nothing but coarse grasses grew;
But such a blast, my King, began to blow,
So loud a blast along the shore and sea,
Ye could not hear the waters for the blast,

Tho' heapt in mounds and ridges all the sea
Drove like a cataract, and all the sand
Swept like a river, and the clouded heavens
Were shaken with the motion and the sound.
And blackening in the sea-foam sway'd a boat,
Half-swallow'd in it, anchor'd with a chain;
And in my madness to myself I said,
"I will embark and I will lose myself,
And in the great sea wash away my sin."
I burst the chain, I sprang into the boat.
Seven days I drove along the dreary deep,
And with me drove the moon and all the stars;
And the wind fell, and on the seventh night
I heard the shingle grinding in the surge,
And felt the boat shock earth, and looking up,
Behold, the enchanted towers of Carbonek,
A castle like a rock upon a rock,
With chasm-like portals open to the sea,

And steps that met the breaker! there was none
Stood near it but a lion on each side
That kept the entry, and the moon was full.
Then from the boat I leapt, and up the stairs.
There drew my sword. With sudden-flaring manes
Those two great beasts rose upright like a man,
Each gript a shoulder, and I stood between;
And, when I would have smitten them, heard a
   voice,
"Doubt not, go forward; if thou doubt, the beasts
Will tear thee piecemeal." Then with violence
The sword was dash'd from out my hand, and fell.
And up into the sounding hall I past;
But nothing in the sounding hall I saw
No bench nor table, painting on the wall
Or shield of knight; only the rounded moon
Thro' the tall oriel on the rolling sea.
But always in the quiet house I heard,

Clear as a lark, high o'er me as a lark,
A sweet voice singing in the topmost tower
To the eastward: up I climb'd a thousand steps
With pain: as in a dream I seem'd to climb
For ever: at the last I reach'd a door,
A light was in the crannies, and I heard,
"Glory and joy and honour to our Lord
And to the Holy Vessel of the Grail."
Then in my madness I essay'd the door;
It gave; and thro' a stormy glare, a heat
As from a seventimes-heated furnace, I,
Blasted and burnt, and blinded as I was,
With such a fierceness that I swoon'd away—
O, yet methought I saw the Holy Grail,
All pall'd in crimson samite, and around
Great angels, awful shapes, and wings and eyes.
And but for all my madness and my sin,
And then my swooning, I had sworn I saw

That which I saw; but what I saw was veil'd
And cover'd; and this quest was not for me.'

"So speaking, and here ceasing, Lancelot left
The hall long silent, till Sir Gawain—nay,
Brother, I need not tell thee foolish words,—
A reckless and irreverent knight was he,
Now bolden'd by the silence of his King,—
Well, I will tell thee: 'O king, my liege,' he said,
'Hath Gawain fail'd in any quest of thine?
When have I stinted stroke in foughten field?
But as for thine, my good friend, Percivale,
Thy holy nun and thou have driven men mad,
Yea, made our mightiest madder than our least.
But by mine eyes and by mine ears I swear,
I will be deafer than the blue-eyed cat,
And thrice as blind as any noonday owl,

To holy virgins in their ecstacies,
Henceforward.'

    "'Deafer,' said the blameless King,
'Gawain, and blinder unto holy things
Hope not to make thyself by idle vows,
Being too blind to have desire to see.
But if indeed there came a sign from heaven,
Blessed are Bors, Lancelot and Percivale,
For these have seen according to their sight.
For every fiery prophet in old times,
And all the sacred madness of the bard,
When God made music thro' them, could but speak
His music by the framework and the chord;
And as ye saw it ye have spoken truth.

    "'Nay—but thou errest, Lancelot: never yet
Could all of true and noble in knight and man

Twine round one sin, whatever it might be,
With such a closeness, but apart there grew,
Save that he were the swine thou spakest of,
Some root of knighthood and pure nobleness;
Whereto see thou, that it may bear its flower.

"'And spake I not too truly, O my knights?
Was I too dark a prophet when I said
To those who went upon the Holy Quest,
That most of them would follow wandering fires,
Lost in the quagmire?—lost to me and gone,
And left me gazing at a barren board,
And a lean Order—scarce return'd a tithe—
And out of those to whom the vision came
My greatest hardly will believe he saw;
Another hath beheld it afar off,
And leaving human wrongs to right themselves,
Cares but to pass into the silent life.

And one hath had the vision face to face,
And now his chair desires him here in vain,
However they may crown him otherwhere.

"'And some among you held, that if the King
Had seen the sight he would have sworn the vow:
Not easily, seeing that the King must guard
That which he rules, and is but as the hind
To whom a space of land is given to plough,
Who may not wander from the allotted field,
Before his work be done; but, being done,
Let visions of the night or of the day
Come, as they will; and many a time they come,
Until this earth he walks on seems not earth,
This light that strikes his eyeball is not light,
This air that smites his forehead is not air
But vision—yea, his very hand and foot—
In moments when he feels he cannot die,

And knows himself no vision to himself,
Nor the high God a vision, nor that One
Who rose again: ye have seen what ye have seen.'

"So spake the king: I knew not all he meant."

PELLEAS AND ETTARRE.

PELLEAS AND ETTARRE.

KING Arthur made new knights to fill the gap
Left by the Holy Quest; and as he sat
In hall at old Caerleon, the high doors
Were softly sunder'd, and thro' these a youth,
Pelleas, and the sweet smell of the fields
Past, and the sunshine came along with him.

"Make me thy knight, because I know, Sir King,
All that belongs to knighthood, and I love,"
Such was his cry; for having heard the King
Had let proclaim a tournament—the prize

A golden circlet and a knightly sword,
Full fain had Pelleas for his lady won
The golden circlet, for himself the sword:
And there were those who knew him near the King
And promised for him: and Arthur made him knight.

And this new knight, Sir Pelleas of the isles—
But lately come to his inheritance,
And lord of many a barren isle was he—
Riding at noon, a day or twain before,
Across the forest call'd of Dean, to find
Caerleon and the King, had felt the sun
Beat like a strong knight on his helm, and reel'd
Almost to falling from his horse; but saw
Near him a mound of even-sloping side,
Whereon a hundred stately beeches grew,
And here and there great hollies under them.
But for a mile all round was open space,

And fern and heath: and slowly Pelleas drew
To that dim day, then binding his good horse
To a tree, cast himself down; and as he lay
At random looking over the brown earth
Thro' that green-glooming twilight of the grove,
It seem'd to Pelleas that the fern without
Burnt as a living fire of emeralds,
So that his eyes were dazzled looking at it.
Then o'er it crost the dimness of a cloud
Floating, and once the shadow of a bird
Flying, and then a fawn; and his eyes closed.
And since he loved all maidens, but no maid
In special, half-awake he whisper'd, "Where?
O where! I love thee, tho' I know thee not.
For fair thou art and pure as Guinevere,
And I will make thee with my spear and sword
As famous—O my queen, my Guinevere,
For I will be thine Arthur when we meet."

Suddenly waken'd with a sound of talk
And laughter at the limit of the wood,
And glancing thro' the hoary boles, he saw,
Strange as to some old prophet might have seem'd
A vision hovering on a sea of fire,
Damsels in divers colours like the cloud
Of sunset and sunrise, and all of them
On horses, and the horses richly trapt
Breast-high in that bright line of bracken stood:
And all the damsels talk'd confusedly,
And one was pointing this way, and one that,
Because the way was lost.

                        And Pelleas rose,
And loosed his horse, and led him to the light.
There she that seem'd the chief among them said,
"In happy time behold our pilot-star!
Youth, we are damsels-errant, and we ride,

Arm'd as ye see, to tilt against the knights
There at Caerleon, but have lost our way:
To right? to left? straight forward? back again?
Which? tell us quickly."

       And Pelleas gazing thought,
"Is Guinevere herself so beautiful?"
For large her violet eyes look'd, and her bloom
A rosy dawn kindled in stainless heavens,
And round her limbs, mature in womanhood,
And slender was her hand and small her shape,
And but for those large eyes, the haunts of scorn,
She might have seem'd a toy to trifle with,
And pass and care no more. But while he gazed
The beauty of her flesh abash'd the boy,
As tho' it were the beauty of her soul:
For as the base man, judging of the good,
Puts his own baseness in him by default

Of will and nature, so did Pelleas lend
All the young beauty of his own soul to hers,
Believing her; and when she spake to him,
Stammer'd, and could not make her a reply.
For out of the waste islands had he come,
Where saving his own sisters he had known
Scarce any but the women of his isles,
Rough wives, that laugh'd and scream'd against the
      gulls,
Makers of nets, and living from the sea.

  Then with a slow smile turn'd the lady round
And look'd upon her people; and as when
A stone is flung into some sleeping tarn,
The circle widens till it lip the marge,
Spread the slow smile thro' all her company.
Three knights were thereamong; and they too smiled,
Scorning him; for the lady was Ettarre,

And she was a great lady in her land.

Again she said, "O wild and of the woods,
Knowest thou not the fashion of our speech?
Or have the Heavens but given thee a fair face,
Lacking a tongue?"

"O damsel," answer'd he,
"I woke from dreams; and coming out of gloom
Was dazzled by the sudden light, and crave
Pardon: but will ye to Caerleon? I
Go likewise: shall I lead you to the King?"

"Lead then," she said; and thro' the woods they went
And while they rode, the meaning in his eyes,
His tenderness of manner, and chaste awe,
His broken utterances and bashfulness,

Were all a burthen to her, and in her heart
She mutter'd, "I have lighted on a fool,
Raw, yet so stale!" But since her mind was bent
On hearing, after trumpet blown, her name
And title, "Queen of Beauty," in the lists
Cried—and beholding him so strong, she thought
That peradventure he will fight for me,
And win the circlet: therefore flatter'd him,
Being so gracious, that he well-nigh deem'd
His wish by hers was echo'd; and her knights
And all her damsels too were gracious to him,
For she was a great lady.

      And when they reach'd
Caerleon, ere they past to lodging, she,
Taking his hand, "O the strong hand," she said,
"See! look at mine! but wilt thou fight for me,
And win me this fine circlet, Pelleas,

That I may love thee!"

       Then his helpless heart
Leapt, and he cried "Ay! wilt thou if I win!"
"Ay, that will I," she answer'd, and she laugh'd,
And straitly nipt the hand, and flung it from her;
Then glanced askew at those three knights of hers,
Till all her ladies laugh'd along with her.

 "O happy world," thought Pelleas, "all, meseems,
Are happy; I the happiest of them all."
Nor slept that night for pleasure in his blood,
And green wood-ways, and eyes among the leaves;
Then being on the morrow knighted, sware
To love one only. And as he came away,
The men who met him rounded on their heels
And wonder'd after him, because his face
Shone like the countenance of a priest of old

Against the flame about a sacrifice
Kindled by fire from heaven: so glad was he.

  Then Arthur made vast banquets, and strange knights
From the four winds came in: and each one sat,
Tho' served with choice from air, land, stream, and sea,
Oft in mid-banquet measuring with his eyes
His neighbour's make and might: and Pelleas look'd
Noble among the noble, for he dream'd
His lady loved him, and he knew himself
Loved of the King: and him his new-made knight
Worshipt, whose lightest whisper moved him more
Than all the ranged reasons of the world.

  Then blush'd and brake the morning of the jousts,
And this was call'd "The Tournament of Youth:"

For Arthur, loving his young knight, withheld
His older and his mightier from the lists,
That Pelleas might obtain his lady's love,
According to her promise, and remain
Lord of the tourney. And Arthur had the jousts
Down in the flat field by the shore of Usk
Holden: the gilded parapets were crown'd
With faces, and the great tower fill'd with eyes
Up to the summit, and the trumpets blew.
There all day long Sir Pelleas kept the field
With honour: so by that strong hand of his
The sword and golden circlet were achieved.

Then rang the shout his lady loved: the heat
Of pride and glory fired her face; her eye
Sparkled; she caught the circlet from his lance,
And there before the people crown'd herself:
So for the last time she was gracious to him.

Then at Caerleon for a space—her look
Bright for all others, cloudier on her knight—
Linger'd Ettarre: and seeing Pelleas droop,
Said Guinevere, "We marvel at thee much,
O damsel, wearing this unsunny face
To him who won thee glory!" And she said,
"Had ye not held your Lancelot in your bower,
My Queen, he had not won." Whereat the Queen,
As one whose foot is bitten by an ant,
Glanced down upon her, turn'd and went her way.

But after, when her damsels, and herself,
And those three knights all set their faces home,
Sir Pelleas follow'd. She that saw him cried,
"Damsels—and yet I should be shamed to say it—
I cannot bide Sir Baby. Keep him back
Among yourselves. Would rather that we had
Some rough old knight who knew the worldly way,

Albeit grizzlier than a bear, to ride
And jest with: take him to you, keep him off,
And pamper him with papmeat, if ye will,
Old milky fables of the wolf and sheep,
Such as the wholesome mothers tell their boys.
Nay, should ye try him with a merry one
To find his mettle, good: and if he fly us,
Small matter! let him." This her damsels heard,
And mindful of her small and cruel hand,
They closing round him thro' the journey home,
Acted her hest, and always from her side
Restrain'd him with all manner of device,
So that he could not come to speech with her.
And when she gain'd her castle, upsprang the bridge,
Down rang the grate of iron thro' the groove,
And he was left alone in open field.

"These be the ways of ladies," Pelleas thought,

"To those who love them, trials of our faith.
Yea, let her prove me to the uttermost,
For loyal to the uttermost am I."
So made his moan; and, darkness falling, sought
A priory not far off, there lodged, but rose
With morning every day, and, moist or dry,
Full-arm'd upon his charger all day long
Sat by the walls, and no one open'd to him.

And this persistance turn'd her scorn to wrath.
Then calling her three knights, she charged them,
"Out!
And drive him from the walls." And out they came,
But Pelleas overthrew them as they dash'd
Against him one by one; and these return'd,
But still he kept his watch beneath the wall.

Thereon her wrath became a hate; and once,

A week beyond, while walking on the walls
With her three knights, she pointed downward, "Look,
He haunts me—I cannot breathe—besieges me;
Down! strike him! put my hate into your strokes,
And drive him from my walls." And down they went,
And Pelleas overthrew them one by one;
And from the tower above him cried Ettarre,
"Bind him, and bring him in."

He heard her voice;
Then let the strong hand, which had overthrown
Her minion-knights, by those he overthrew
Be bounden straight, and so they brought him in.

Then when he came before Ettarre, the sight
Of her rich beauty made him at one glance
More bondsman in his heart than in his bonds.
Yet with good cheer he spake, "Behold me, Lady,

A prisoner, and the vassal of thy will;
And if thou keep me in thy donjon here,
Content am I so that I see thy face
But once a day: for I have sworn my vows,
And thou hast given thy promise, and I know
That all these pains are trials of my faith,
And that thyself when thou hast seen me strain'd
And sifted to the utmost, wilt at length
Yield me thy love and know me for thy knight."

Then she began to rail so bitterly,
With all her damsels, he was stricken mute;
But when she mock'd his vows and the great
        King,
Lighted on words: "For pity of thine own self,
Peace, Lady, peace: is he not thine and mine?"
"Thou fool," she said, "I never heard his voice
But long'd to break away. Unbind him now,

And thrust him out of doors; for save he be
Fool to the midmost marrow of his bones,
He will return no more." And those, her three,
Laugh'd, and unbound, and thrust him from the
   gate.

And after this, a week beyond, again
She call'd them, saying, "There he watches yet,
There like a dog before his master's door!
Kick'd, he returns: do ye not hate him, ye?
Ye know yourselves: how can ye bide at peace,
Affronted with his fulsome innocence?
Are ye but creatures of the board and bed,
No men to strike? Fall on him all at once,
And if ye slay him I reck not: if ye fail,
Give ye the slave mine order to be bound,
Bind him as heretofore, and bring him in:
It may be ye shall slay him in his bonds.

She spake; and at her will they couch'd their
    spears,
Three against one: and Gawain passing by,
Bound upon solitary adventure, saw
Low down beneath the shadow of those towers
A villainy, three to one: and thro' his heart
The fire of honour and all noble deeds
Flash'd, and he call'd, "I strike upon thy side—
The caitiffs!" "Nay," said Pelleas, "but forbear;
He needs no aid who doth his lady's will."

So Gawain, looking at the villainy done,
Forbore, but in his heat and eagerness
Trembled and quiver'd, as the dog, withheld
A moment from the vermin that he sees
Before him, shivers, ere he springs and kills.

And Pelleas overthrew them, one to three;

And they rose up, and bound, and brought him in.
Then first her anger, leaving Pelleas, burn'd
Full on her knights in many an evil name
Of craven, weakling, and thrice-beaten hound:
"Yet, take him, ye that scarce are fit to touch,
Far less to bind, your victor, and thrust him out,
And let who will release him from his bonds.
And if he comes again"—there she brake short;
And Pelleas answer'd, "Lady, for indeed
I loved you and I deem'd you beautiful,
I cannot brook to see your beauty marr'd
Thro' evil spite: and if ye love me not,
I cannot bear to dream you so forsworn:
I had liefer ye were worthy of my love,
Than to be loved again of you—farewell;
And tho' ye kill my hope, not yet my love,
Vex not yourself: ye will not see me more."

While thus he spake, she gazed upon the man
Of princely bearing, tho' in bonds, and thought,
"Why have I push'd him from me? this man loves,
If love there be: yet him I loved not. Why?
I deem'd him fool? yea, so? or that in him
A something—was it nobler than myself?—
Seem'd my reproach? He is not of my kind.
He could not love me, did he know me well.
Nay, let him go—and quickly." And her knights
Laugh'd not, but thrust him bounden out of door.

Forth sprang Gawain, and loosed him from his bonds,
And flung them o'er the walls; and afterward,
Shaking his hands, as from a lazar's rag,
"Faith of my body," he said, "and art thou not—
Yea thou art he, whom late our Arthur made
Knight of his table; yea and he that won
The circlet? wherefore hast thou so defamed

Thy brotherhood in me and all the rest,
As let these caitiffs on thee work their will?"

And Pelleas answer'd, "O, their wills are hers,
For whom I won the circlet; and mine, hers,
Thus to be bounden, so to see her face,
Marr'd tho' it be with spite and mockery now,
Other than when I found her in the woods;
And tho' she hath me bounden but in spite,
And all to flout me, when they bring me in,
Let me be bounden, I shall see her face;
Else must I die thro' mine unhappiness."

And Gawain answer'd kindly tho' in scorn,
"Why, let my lady bind me if she will,
And let my lady beat me if she will:
But an she send her delegate to thrall
These fighting hands of mine—Christ kill me then

But I will slice him handless by the wrist,
And let my lady sear the stump for him,
Howl as he may. But hold me for your friend:
Come, ye know nothing: here I pledge my troth,
Yea, by the honour of the Table Round,
I will be leal to thee and work thy work,
And tame thy jailing princess to thine hand.
Lend me thine horse and arms, and I will say
That I have slain thee. She will let me in
To hear the manner of thy fight and fall;
Then, when I come within her counsels, then
From prime to vespers will I chant thy praise
As prowest knight and truest lover, more
Than any have sung thee living, till she long
To have thee back in lusty life again,
Not to be bound, save by white bonds and warm,
Dearer than freedom. Wherefore now thy horse
And armour: let me go: be comforted:

Give me three days to melt her fancy, and hope
The third night hence will bring thee news of
gold."

Then Pelleas lent his horse and all his arms,
Saving the goodly sword, his prize, and took
Gawain's, and said "Betray me not, but help—
Art thou not he whom men call light-of-love?"

"Ay," said Gawain, "for women be so light."
Then bounded forward to the castle walls,
And raised a bugle hanging from his neck,
And winded it, and that so musically
That all the old echoes hidden in the wall
Rang out like hollow woods at huntingtide.

Up ran a score of damsels to the tower;
"Avaunt," they cried, "our lady loves thee not."

But Gawain lifting up his visor said,
"Gawain am I, Gawain of Arthur's court,
And I have slain this Pelleas whom ye hate:
Behold his horse and armour. Open gate,
And I will make you merry."

                                            And down they ran,
Her damsels, crying to their lady, "Lo!
Pelleas is dead—he told us—he that hath
His horse and armour: will ye let him in?
He slew him! Gawain, Gawain of the court,
Sir Gawain—there he waits below the wall,
Blowing his bugle as who should say him nay."

And so, leave given, straight on thro' open door
Rode Gawain, whom she greeted courteously.
"Dead, is it so?" she ask'd. "Ay, ay," said he,
"And oft in dying cried upon your name."

"Pity on him," she answer'd, "a good knight,
But never let me bide one hour at peace."
"Ay," thought Gawain, "and ye be fair enow:
But I to your dead man have given my troth,
That whom ye loathe him will I make you love."

So those three days, aimless about the land,
Lost in a doubt, Pelleas wandering
Waited, until the third night brought a moon
With promise of large light on woods and ways.

The night was hot: he could not rest, but rode
Ere midnight to her walls, and bound his horse
Hard by the gates. Wide open were the gates,
And no watch kept; and in thro' these he past,
And heard but his own steps, and his own heart
Beating, for nothing moved but his own self,
And his own shadow. Then he crost the court,

And saw the postern portal also wide
Yawning; and up a slope of garden, all
Of roses white and red, and wild ones mixt
And overgrowing them, went on, and found,
Here too, all hush'd below the mellow moon,
Save that one rivulet from a tiny cave
Came lightening downward, and so spilt itself
Among the roses, and was lost again.

Then was he ware that white pavilions rose,
Three from the bushes, gilden-peakt: in one,
Red after revel, droned her lurdane knights
Slumbering, and their three squires across their
    feet:
In one, their malice on the placid lip
Froz'n by sweet sleep, four of her damsels lay:
And in the third, the circlet of the jousts
Bound on her brow, were Gawain and Ettarre.

Back, as a hand that pushes thro' the leaf
To find a nest and feels a snake, he drew:
Back, as a coward slinks from what he fears
To cope with, or a traitor proven, or hound
Beaten, did Pelleas in an utter shame
Creep with his shadow thro' the court again,
Fingering at his sword-handle until he stood
There on the castle-bridge once more, and thought,
"I will go back, and slay them where they lie."

And so went back and seeing them yet in sleep
Said, "Ye, that so dishallow the holy sleep,
Your sleep is death," and drew the sword, and thought,
"What! slay a sleeping knight? the King hath bound
And sworn me to this brotherhood;" again,
"Alas that ever a knight should be so false."
Then turn'd, and so return'd, and groaning laid
The naked sword athwart their naked throats,

There left it, and them sleeping; and she lay,
The circlet of the tourney round her brows,
And the sword of the tourney across her throat.

And forth he past, and mounting on his horse
Stared at her towers that, larger than themselves
In their own darkness, throng'd into the moon.
Then crush'd the saddle with his thighs, and clench'd
His hands, and madden'd with himself and moan'd:

"Would they have risen against me in their blood
At the last day? I might have answer'd them
Even before high God. O towers so strong,
Huge, solid, would that even while I gaze
The crack of earthquake shivering to your base
Split you, and Hell burst up your harlot roofs
Bellowing, and charr'd you thro' and thro' within,

Black as the harlot's heart—hollow as a skull!
Let the fierce east scream thro' your eyelet-holes,
And whirl the dust of harlots round and round
In dung and nettles! hiss, snake—I saw him there—
Let the fox bark, let the wolf yell. Who yells
Here in the still sweet summer night, but I—
I, the poor Pelleas whom she call'd her fool?
Fool, beast—he, she, or I? myself most fool;
Beast too, as lacking human wit—disgraced,
Dishonour'd all for trial of true love—
Love?—we be all alike: only the king
Hath made us fools and liars. O noble vows!
O great and sane and simple race of brutes
That own no lust because they have no law!
For why should I have loved her to my shame?
I loathe her, as I loved her to my shame.
I never loved her, I but lusted for her—
Away—"

He dash'd the rowel into his horse,
And bounded forth and vanish'd thro' the night.

Then she, that felt the cold touch on her throat,
Awaking knew the sword, and turn'd herself
To Gawain: "Liar, for thou hast not slain
This Pelleas! here he stood and might have slain
Me and thyself." And he that tells the tale
Says that her ever-veering fancy turn'd
To Pelleas, as the one true knight on earth,
And only lover; and thro' her love her life
Wasted and pined, desiring him in vain.

But he by wild and way, for half the night,
And over hard and soft, striking the sod
From out the soft, the spark from off the hard,
Rode till the star above the wakening sun,
Beside that tower where Percivale was cowl'd,

Glanced from the rosy forehead of the dawn.
For so the words were flash'd into his heart
He knew not whence or wherefore: "O sweet star,
Pure on the virgin forehead of the dawn."
And there he would have wept, but felt his eyes
Harder and drier than a fountain bed
In summer: thither came the village girls
And linger'd talking, and they come no more
Till the sweet heavens have fill'd it from the heights
Again with living waters in the change
Of seasons: hard his eyes; harder his heart
Seem'd; but so weary were his limbs, that he,
Gasping, "Of Arthur's hall am I, but here,
Here let me rest and die," cast himself down,
And gulph'd his griefs in inmost sleep; so lay,
Till shaken by a dream, that Gawain fired
The hall of Merlin, and the morning star
Reel'd in the smoke, brake into flame, and fell.

He woke, and being ware of some one nigh,
Sent hands upon him, as to tear him, crying
"False! and I held thee pure as Guinevere."

But Percivale stood near him and replied,
"Am I but false as Guinevere is pure?
Or art thou mazed with dreams? or being one
Of our free-spoken Table hast not heard
That Lancelot"—there he check'd himself and paused.

Then fared it with Sir Pelleas as with one
Who gets a wound in battle, and the sword
That made it plunges thro' the wound again,
And pricks it deeper: and he shrank and wail'd,
"Is the Queen false?" and Percivale was mute.
"Have any of our Round Table held their vows?"
And Percivale made answer not a word.
"Is the king true?" "The king!" said Percivale.

"Why then let men couple at once with wolves.
What! art thou mad!"

                    But Pelleas, leaping up,
Ran thro' the doors and vaulted on his horse
And fled: small pity upon his horse had he,
Or on himself, or any, and when he met
A cripple, one that held a hand for alms—
Hunch'd as he was, and like an old dwarf-elm
That turns its back on the salt blast, the boy
Paused not but overrode him, shouting "False,
And false with Gawain!" and so left him bruised
And batter'd, and fled on, and hill and wood
Went ever streaming by him till the gloom,
That follows on the turning of the world,
Darken'd the common path: he twitch'd the reins,
And made his beast that better knew it, swerve
Now off it and now on; but when he saw

High up in heaven the hall that Merlin built,
Blackening against the dead-green stripes of even,
"Black nest of rats," he groan'd, "ye build too high."

    Not long thereafter from the city gates
Issued Sir Lancelot riding airily,
Warm with a gracious parting from the Queen,
Peace at his heart, and gazing at a star
And marvelling what it was: on whom the boy,
Across the silent seeded meadow-grass
Borne, clash'd: and Lancelot, saying, "What name hast thou
That ridest here so blindly and so hard?"
"I have no name," he shouted, "a scourge am I,
To lash the treasons of the Table Round."
"Yea, but thy name?" "I have many names," he cried:
"I am wrath and shame and hate and evil fame,
And like a poisonous wind I pass to blast

And blaze the crime of Lancelot and the Queen."
"First over me," said Lancelot, "shalt thou pass."
"Fight therefore," yell'd the other, and either knight
Drew back a space, and when they closed, at once
The weary steed of Pelleas floundering flung
His rider, who called out from the dark field,
"Thou art false as Hell: slay me: I have no sword."
Then Lancelot, "Yea, between thy lips—and sharp;
But here will I disedge it by thy death."
"Slay then," he shriek'd, "my will is to be slain."
And Lancelot, with his heel upon the fall'n,
Rolling his eyes, a moment stood, then spake:
"Rise, weakling; I am Lancelot; say thy say."

And Lancelot slowly rode his war-horse back
To Camelot, and Sir Pelleas in brief while
Caught his unbroken limbs from the dark field,
And follow'd to the city. It chanced that both

Brake into hall together, worn and pale.
There with her knights and dames was Guinevere.
Full wonderingly she gazed on Lancelot
So soon return'd, and then on Pelleas, him
Who had not greeted her, but cast himself
Down on a bench, hard-breathing. "Have ye fought?"
She ask'd of Lancelot. "Ay, my Queen," he said.
"And thou hast overthrown him?" "Ay, my Queen."
Then she, turning to Pelleas, "O young knight,
Hath the great heart of knighthood in thee fail'd
So far thou canst not bide, unfrowardly,
A fall from him?" Then, for he answer'd not,
"Or hast thou other griefs? If I, the Queen,
May help them, loose thy tongue, and let me know."
But Pelleas lifted up an eye so fierce
She quail'd; and he, hissing "I have no sword,"
Sprang from the door into the dark. The Queen
Look'd hard upon her lover, he on her;

And each foresaw the dolorous day to be:
And all talk died, as in a grove all song
Beneath the shadow of some bird of prey.
Then a long silence came upon the hall,
And Modred thought, "The time is hard at hand."

THE PASSING OF ARTHUR.

THE PASSING OF ARTHUR.

THAT story which the bold Sir Bedivère,
First made and latest left of all the knights,
Told, when the man was no more than a voice
In the white winter of his age, to those
With whom he dwelt, new faces, other minds.

Before that last weird battle in the west
There came on Arthur sleeping, Gawain kill'd
In Lancelot's war, the ghost of Gawain blown
Along a wandering wind, and past his ear
Went shrilling "Hollow, hollow all delight!

Hail, king! to-morrow thou shalt pass away.
Farewell! there is an isle of rest for thee.
And I am blown along a wandering wind,
And hollow, hollow, hollow all delight."
And fainter onward, like wild birds that change
Their season in the night and wail their way
From cloud to cloud, down the long wind the
   dream
Shrill'd; but in going mingled with dim cries
Far in the moonlit haze among the hills,
As of some lonely city sack'd by night,
When all is lost, and wife and child with wail
Pass to new lords; and Arthur woke and call'd,
"Who spake? A dream. O light upon the wind,
Thine, Gawain, was the voice—are these dim cries
Thine? or doth all that haunts the waste and
   wild
Mourn, knowing it will go along with me?"

This heard the bold Sir Bedivere and spake:
"O me, my king, let pass whatever will,
Elves, and the harmless glamour of the field;
But in their stead thy name and glory cling
To all high places like a golden cloud
For ever: but as yet thou shalt not pass.
Light was Gawain in life, and light in death
Is Gawain, for the ghost is as the man;
And care not thou for dreams from him, but
    rise—
I hear the steps of Modred in the west,
And with him many of thy people, and knights
Once thine, whom thou hast loved, but grosser grown
Than heathen, spitting at their vows and thee.
Right well in heart they know thee for the King.
Arise, go forth and conquer as of old."

Then spake King Arthur to Sir Bedivere:

"Far other is this battle in the west
Whereto we move, than when we strove in youth,
And thrust the heathen from the Roman wall,
And shook him thro' the north. Ill doom is mine
To war against my people and my knights.
The king who fights his people fights himself.
And they my knights, who loved me once, the
    stroke
That strikes them dead is as my death to me.
Yet let us hence, and find or feel a way
Thro' this blind haze, which ever since I saw
One lying in the dust at Almesbury,
Hath folded in the passes of the world."

Then rose the King and moved his host by night,
And ever push'd Sir Modred, league by league,
Back to the sunset bound of Lyonnesse—
A land of old upheaven from the abyss

By fire, to sink into the abyss again;
Where fragments of forgotten peoples dwelt,
And the long mountains ended in a coast
Of ever-shifting sand, and far away
The phantom circle of a moaning sea.
There the pursuer could pursue no more,
And he that fled no further fly the King;
And there, that day when the great light of heaven
Burn'd at his lowest in the rolling year,
On the waste sand by the waste sea they closed.
Nor ever yet had Arthur fought a fight
Like this last, dim, weird battle of the west.
A deathwhite mist slept over sand and sea:
Whereof the chill, to him who breathed it, drew
Down with his blood, till all his heart was cold
With formless fear; and ev'n on Arthur fell
Confusion, since he saw not whom he fought,
For friend and foe were shadows in the mist,

And friend slew friend not knowing whom he slew;
And some had visions out of golden youth,
And some beheld the faces of old ghosts
Look in upon the battle; and in the mist
Was many a noble deed, many a base,
And chance and craft and strength in single fights,
And ever and anon with host to host
Shocks, and the splintering spear, the hard mail
      hewn,
Shield-breakings, and the clash of brands, the crash
Of battleaxes on shatter'd helms, and shrieks
After the Christ, of those who falling down
Looked up for heaven, and only saw the mist;
And shouts of heathen and the traitor knights,
Oaths, insult, filth, and monstrous blasphemies,
Sweat, writhings, anguish, labouring of the lungs
In that close mist, and cryings for the light,
Moans of the dying, and voices of the dead,

Last, as by some one deathbed after wail
Of suffering, silence follows, or thro' death
Or deathlike swoon, thus over all that shore,
Save for some whisper of the seething seas,
A dead hush fell; but when the dolorous day
Grew drearier toward twilight falling, came
A bitter wind, clear from the North, and blew
The mist aside, and with that wind the tide
Rose, and the pale king glanced across the field
Of battle: but no man was moving there;
Nor any cry of Christian heard thereon,
Nor yet of heathen; only the wan wave
Brake in among dead faces, to and fro
Swaying the helpless hands, and up and down
Tumbling the hollow helmets, of the fallen,
And shiver'd brands that once had fought with Rome,
And rolling far along the gloomy shores
The voice of days of old and days to be.

Then spake King Arthur to Sir Bedivere,
And whiter than the mist that all day long
Had held the field of battle was the King:

"Hearest thou this great voice that shakes the world,
And wastes the narrow realm whereon we move,
And beats upon the faces of the dead,
My dead, as tho' they had not died for me?—
O Bedivere, for on my heart hath fall'n
Confusion, till I know not what I am,
Nor whence I am, nor whether I be king.
Behold, I seem but king among the dead."

Then spake the bold Sir Bedivere: "My King,
King everywhere! and so the dead have kings,
There also will I worship thee as king.
Yet still thy life is whole, and still I live
Who love thee; but who hates thee, he that brought

The heathen back among us, yonder stands,
Modred; unharm'd, the traitor of thine house."

Then spake the King: "My house hath been my
    doom.
But call not thou this traitor of my house
Who hath but dwelt beneath one roof with me.
My house are rather they who sware my vows,
Yea, even while they brake them, own'd me king.
And well for thee, saying in my dark hour,
When all the purport of my throne hath fail'd,
That quick or dead thou holdest me for king.
King am I, whatsoever be their cry
And one last act of kinghood shalt thou see
Yet, ere I pass." And uttering this the king
Made at the man: then Modred smote his liege
Hard on that helm which many a heathen sword
Had beaten thin; while Arthur at one blow,

Striking the last stroke with Excalibur,
Slew him, and all but slain himself, he fell.

So all day long the noise of battle roll'd
Among the mountains by the winter sea;
Until King Arthur's Table, man by man,
Had fall'n in Lyonnesse about their lord,
King Arthur. Then, because his wound was
    deep,
The bold Sir Bedivere uplifted him,
And bore him to a chapel nigh the field,
A broken chancel with a broken cross,
That stood on a dark strait of barren land:
On one side lay the Ocean, and on one
Lay a great water, and the moon was full.

Then spake King Arthur to Sir Bedivere:
"The sequel of to-day unsolders all

The goodliest fellowship of famous knights
Whereof this world holds record. Such a sleep
They sleep—the men I loved. I think that we
Shall never more, at any future time,
Delight our souls with talk of knightly deeds,
Walking about the gardens and the halls
Of Camelot, as in the days that were.
I perish by this people which I made,—
Tho' Merlin sware that I should come again
To rule once more; but let what will be, be.
I am so deeply smitten thro' the helm,
That without help I cannot last till morn.
Thou therefore take my brand Excalibur,
Which was my pride: for thou rememberest how
In those old days, one summer noon, an arm
Rose up from out the bosom of the lake,
Clothed in white samite, mystic, wonderful,
Holding the sword—and how I row'd across

And took it, and have worn it, like a king;
And, wheresoever I am sung or told
In aftertime, this also shall be known:
But now delay not: take Excalibur,
And fling him far into the middle mere:
Watch what thou seëst, and lightly bring me
  word."

To him replied the bold Sir Bedivere:
"It is not meet, Sir King, to leave thee thus,
Aidless, alone, and smitten thro' the helm—
A little thing may harm a wounded man;
Yet I thy hest will all perform at full,
Watch what I see, and lightly bring thee word."

So saying, from the ruin'd shrine he stept,
And in the moon athwart the place of tombs,
Where lay the mighty bones of ancient men,

Old knights, and over them the sea-wind sang
Shrill, chill, with flakes of foam. He, stepping down
By zig-zag paths, and juts of pointed rock,
Came on the shining levels of the lake.

There drew he forth the brand Excalibur,
And o'er him, drawing it, the winter moon,
Brightening the skirts of a long cloud, ran forth
And sparkled keen with frost against the hilt:
For all the haft twinkled with diamond sparks,
Myriads of topaz-lights, and jacinth-work
Of subtlest jewelry. He gazed so long
That both his eyes were dazzled as he stood,
This way and that dividing the swift mind,
In act to throw: but at the last it seem'd
Better to leave Excalibur conceal'd
There in the many-knotted waterflags,
That whistled stiff and dry about the marge.

So strode he back slow to the wounded King.

Then spake King Arthur to Sir Bedivere:
"Hast thou perform'd my mission which I gave?
What is it thou hast seen? or what hast heard?"

And answer made the bold Sir Bedivere:
"I heard the ripple washing in the reeds,
And the wild water lapping on the crag."

To whom replied King Arthur, faint and pale:
"Thou hast betray'd thy nature and thy name,
Not rendering true answer, as beseem'd
Thy fëalty, nor like a noble knight:
For surer sign had follow'd, either hand,
Or voice, or else a motion of the mere.
This is a shameful thing for men to lie.
Yet now, I charge thee, quickly go again,

As thou art lief and dear, and do the thing
I bade thee, watch, and lightly bring me word."

Then went Sir Bedivere the second time
Across the ridge, and paced beside the mere,
Counting the dewy pebbles, fix'd in thought;
But when he saw the wonder of the hilt,
How curiously and strangely chased, he smote
His palms together, and he cried aloud:

"And if indeed I cast the brand away,
Surely a precious thing, one worthy note,
Should thus be lost for ever from the earth,
Which might have pleased the eyes of many men.
What good should follow this, if this were done?
What harm, undone? Deep harm to disobey,
Seeing obedience is the bond of rule.
Were it well to obey then, if a king demand

An act unprofitable, against himself?
The King is sick, and knows not what he does.
What record, or what relic of my lord
Should be to aftertime, but empty breath
And rumours of a doubt? But were this kept,
Stored in some treasure-house of mighty kings,
Some one might show it at a joust of arms,
Saying, 'King Arthur's sword, Excalibur,
Wrought by the lonely maiden of the Lake.
Nine years she wrought it, sitting in the deeps
Upon the hidden bases of the hills.'
So might some old man speak in the aftertime
To all the people, winning reverence.
But now much honour and much fame were lost."

So spake he, clouded with his own conceit,
And hid Excalibur the second time,
And so strode back slow to the wounded King.

Then spoke King Arthur, breathing heavily:
"What is it thou hast seen? or what hast heard?"

And answer made the bold Sir Bedivere:
"I heard the water lapping on the crag,
And the long ripple washing in the reeds."

To whom replied King Arthur, much in wrath:
"Ah, miserable and unkind, untrue,
Unknightly, traitor-hearted! Woe is me!
Authority forgets a dying king,
Laid widow'd of the power in his eye
That bow'd the will. I see thee what thou art,
For thou, the latest-left of all my knights
In whom should meet the offices of all,
Thou wouldst betray me for the precious hilt;
Either from lust of gold, or like a girl
Valuing the giddy pleasure of the eyes.

Yet, for a man may fail in duty twice,
And the third time may prosper, get thee hence:
But, if thou spare to fling Excalibur,
I will arise and slay thee with my hands."

   Then quickly rose Sir Bedivere, and ran,
And, leaping down the ridges lightly, plunged
Among the bulrush-beds, and clutch'd the sword,
And strongly wheel'd and threw it. The great brand
Made lightnings in the splendour of the moon,
And flashing round and round, and whirl'd in an arch,
Shot like a streamer of the northern morn,
Seen where the moving isles of winter shock
By night, with noises of the northern sea.
So flash'd and fell the brand Excalibur:
But ere he dipt the surface, rose an arm
Clothed in white samite, mystic, wonderful,
And caught him by the hilt, and brandish'd him

Three times, and drew him under in the mere.
And lightly went the other to the King.

Then spoke King Arthur, drawing thicker breath:
"Now see I by thine eyes that this is done.
Speak out: what is it thou hast heard, or seen?"

And answer made the bold Sir Bedivere:
"Sir King, I closed mine eyelids, lest the gems
Should blind my purpose, for I never saw,
Nor shall see, here or elsewhere, till I die,
Not tho' I live three lives of mortal men,
So great a miracle as yonder hilt.
Then with both hands I flung him, wheeling him;
But when I look'd again, behold an arm,
Clothed in white samite, mystic, wonderful,
That caught him by the hilt, and brandish'd him
Three times, and drew him under in the mere."

And answer made King Arthur, breathing hard:
"My end draws nigh; 'tis time that I were gone.
Make broad thy shoulders to receive my weight,
And bear me to the margin; yet I fear
My wound hath taken cold, and I shall die."

So saying, from the pavement he half rose,
Slowly, with pain, reclining on his arm,
And looking wistfully with wide blue eyes
As in a picture. Him Sir Bedivere
Remorsefully regarded thro' his tears,
And would have spoken, but he found not words;
Then took with care, and kneeling on one knee,
O'er both his shoulders drew the languid hands,
And rising bore him thro' the place of tombs.

But, as he walk'd, King Arthur panted hard,
Like one that feels a nightmare on his bed

When all the house is mute. So sigh'd the King,
Muttering and murmuring at his ear "Quick, quick!
I fear it is too late, and I shall die."
But the other swiftly strode from ridge to ridge,
Clothed with his breath, and looking, as he walk'd,
Larger than human on the frozen hills.
He heard the deep behind him, and a cry
Before. His own thought drove him like a goad.
Dry clash'd his harness in the icy caves
And barren chasms, and all to left and right
The bare black cliff clang'd round him, as he based
His feet on juts of slippery crag that rang
Sharp-smitten with the dint of armed heels—
And on a sudden, lo! the level lake,
And the long glories of the winter moon.

Then saw they how there hove a dusky barge,
Dark as a funeral scarf from stem to stern,

Beneath them; and descending they were ware
That all the decks were dense with stately forms,
Black-stoled, black-hooded, like a dream—by these
Three Queens with crowns of gold: and from them rose
A cry that shiver'd to the tingling stars,
And, as it were one voice, an agony
Of lamentation, like a wind that shrills
All night in a waste land, where no one comes,
Or hath come, since the making of the world.

Then murmur'd Arthur, "Place me in the barge;"
So to the barge they came. There those three Queens
Put forth their hands, and took the King, and wept.
But she, that rose the tallest of them all
And fairest, laid his head upon her lap,
And loosed the shatter'd casque, and chafed his hands,
And call'd him by his name, complaining loud,
And dropping bitter tears against his brow

Striped with dark blood: for all his face was white
And colourless, and like the wither'd moon
Smote by the fresh beam of the springing east;
And all his greaves and cuisses dash'd with drops
Of onset; and the light and lustrous curls—
That made his forehead like a rising sun
High from the daïs-throne—were parch'd with dust;
Or, clotted into points and hanging loose,
Mix'd with the knightly growth that fringed his lips.
So like a shatter'd column lay the King;
Not like that Arthur who, with lance in rest,
From spur to plume a star of tournament,
Shot thro' the lists at Camelot, and charged
Before the eyes of ladies and of kings.

Then loudly cried the bold Sir Bedivere:
"Ah! my Lord Arthur, whither shall I go?
Where shall I hide my forehead and my eyes?

For now I see the true old times are dead,
When every morning brought a noble chance,
And every chance brought out a noble knight.
Such times have been not since the light that led
The holy Elders with the gift of myrrh.
But now the whole Round Table is dissolved
Which was an image of the mighty world;
And I, the last, go forth companionless,
And the days darken round me, and the years,
Among new men, strange faces, other minds."

And slowly answered Arthur from the barge:
"The old order changeth, yielding place to new,
And God fulfils himself in many ways,
Lest one good custom should corrupt the world.
Comfort thyself: what comfort is in me?
I have lived my life, and that which I have done
May He within himself make pure! but thou,

If thou shouldst never see my face again,
Pray for my soul. More things are wrought by
prayer
Than this world dreams of. Wherefore, let thy
voice
Rise like a fountain for me night and day.
For what are men better than sheep or goats
That nourish a blind life within the brain,
If, knowing God, they lift not hands of prayer
Both for themselves and those who call them friend?
For so the whole round earth is every way
Bound by gold chains about the feet of God.
But now farewell. I am going a long way
With these thou seest—if indeed I go
(For all my mind is clouded with a doubt)—
To the island-valley of Avilion;
Where falls not hail, or rain, or any snow,
Nor ever wind blows loudly; but it lies

Deep-meadow'd, happy, fair with orchard-lawns
And bowery hollows crown'd with summer sea,
Where I will heal me of my grievous wound."

So said he, and the barge with oar and sail
Moved from the brink, like some full-breasted swan
That, fluting a wild carol ere her death,
Ruffles her pure cold plume, and takes the flood
With swarthy webs. Long stood Sir Bedivere
Revolving many memories, till the hull
Look'd one black dot against the verge of dawn,
And on the mere the wailing died away.

At length he groan'd, and turning slowly clomb
The last hard footstep of that iron crag;
Thence mark'd the black hull moving yet, and cried,
"He passes to be king among the dead,
And after healing of his grievous wound

He comes again; but—if he come no more—
O me, be yon dark Queens in yon black boat,
Who shriek'd and wail'd, the three whereat we gazed
On that high day, when, clothed with living light,
They stood before his throne in silence, friends
Of Arthur, who should help him at his need?"

Then from the dawn it seem'd there came, but faint
As from beyond the limit of the world,
Like the last echo born of a great cry,
Sounds, as if some fair city were one voice
Around a king returning from his wars.

Thereat once more he moved about, and clomb
E'en to the highest he could climb, and saw,
Straining his eyes beneath an arch of hand,
Or thought he saw, the speck that bare the king,
Down that long water opening on the deep

Somewhere far off, pass on and on, and go
From less to less and vanish into light.
And the new sun rose bringing the new year.

MISCELLANEOUS.

NORTHERN FARMER.

NEW STYLE.

I.

Dosn't thou 'ear my 'erse's legs, as they canters awaäy?

Proputty, proputty, proputty—that's what I 'ears 'em saäy.

Proputty, proputty, proputty—Sam, thou's an ass for thy paaïns:

Theer's moor sense i' one o' 'is legs nor in all thy braaïns.

II.

Woä—theer's a craw to pluck wi' tha, Sam: yon's parson's 'ouse—

Dosn't thou knaw that a man mun be eäther a man or a mouse?

Time to think on it then; for thou'll be twenty to weeäk.*

Proputty, proputty—woä then woä—let ma 'ear mysén speäk.

III.

Me an' thy muther, Sammy, 'as beän a-talkin' o' thee;

Thou's been talkin' to muther, an' she beän a tellin' it me.

Thou'll not marry for munny—thou's sweet upo' parson's lass—

Noä—thou'll marry fur luvv—an' we boäth on us thinks tha an ass.

* This week.

IV.

Seeä'd her todaäy goä by—Saäint's-daäy—they was
  ringing the bells.
She's a beauty thou thinks—an' soä is scoors o' gells,
Them as 'as munny an' all—wot's a beauty?—the
  flower as blaws.
But proputty, proputty sticks, an' proputty, proputty
  graws.

V.

Do'ant be stunt*: taäke time: I knaws what maäkes
  tha sa mad.
Warn't I craäzed fur the lasses mysén when I wur
  a lad?
But I knaw'd a Quaäker feller as often 'as towd ma
  this:
"Doänt thou marry for munny, but goä wheer munny
  is!"

* Obstinate.

VI.

An' I went wheer munny war: an' thy mother coom
    to 'and,
Wi' lots o' munny laaïd by, an' a nicetish bit o' land.
Maäybe she warn't a beauty:—I niver giv it a
    thowt—
But warn't she as good to cuddle an' kiss as a lass
    as 'ant nowt?

VII.

Parson's lass 'ant nowt, an' she weänt 'a nowt when
    'e's deäd,
Mun be a guvness, lad, or summut, and addle* her
    breäd:
Why? fur 'e's nobbut a curate, an' weänt nivir git
    naw 'igher;
An' 'e maäde the bed as 'e ligs on afoor 'e coom'd
    to the shire.

        * Earn.

VIII.

And thin 'e coom'd to the parish wi' lots o' 'Varsity debt,

Stook to his taaïl they did, an' 'e 'ant got shut on 'em yet.

An' 'e ligs on 'is back i' the grip, wi noän to lend 'im a shove,

Woorse nor a far-welter'd* yowe: fur, Sammy, 'e married fur luvv.

IX.

Luvv! what's luvv? thou can luvv thy lass an' 'er munny too,

Maakin' 'em goä togither as they've good right to do.

Could'n I luvv thy muther by cause o' 'er munny laaïd by?

Naäy—fur I luvv'd 'er a vast sight moor fur it: reäson why.

---

* Or fow-welter'd—said of a sheep lying on its back in the furrow.

X.

Ay an' thy muther says thou wants to marry the lass,
Cooms of a gentleman burn: an' we boäth on us thinks tha an ass.
Woä then, proputty, wiltha?—an ass as near as mays nowt—*
Woä then, wiltha? dangtha!—the bees is as fell as owt.†

XI.

Breäk me a bit o' the esh for his 'eäd, lad, out o' the fence!
Gentleman burn! what's gentleman burn? is it shillins an' pence?
Proputty, proputty's ivrything 'ere, an', Sammy, I'm blest
If it isn't the saäme oop yonder, fur them as 'as it's the best.

* Makes nothing.   † The flies are as fierce as anything.

XII.

Tis'n them as 'as munny as breäks into 'ouses an' steäls,
Them as 'as coäts to their backs an' taäkes their regular meäls.
Noä, but it's them as niver knaws wheer a meäl's to be 'ad.
Taäke my word for it, Sammy, the poor in a loomp is bad.

XIII.

Them or thir feythers, tha sees, mun 'a beän a laäzy lot,
Fur work mun 'a gone to the gittin' whiniver munny was got.
Feyther 'ad ammost nowt; leästwaays 'is munny was 'id.
But 'e tued an' moil'd 'issén deäd, an 'e died a good un, 'e did.

XIV.

Look thou theer wheer Wrigglesby beck comes out
    by the 'ill!
Feyther run up to the farm, an' I runs up to the
    mill;
An' I'll run up to the brig, an' that thou'll live to
    see;
And if thou marries a good un I'll leäve the land
    to thee.

XV.

Thim's my noätions, Sammy, wheerby I means to
    stick;
But if thou marries a bad un, I'll leäve the land to
    Dick.—
Coom oop, proputty, proputty—that's what I 'ears
    'im saäy—
Proputty, proputty, proputty—canter an' canter
    awaäy.

THE GOLDEN SUPPER.

[This poem is founded upon a story in Boccaccio.
A young lover, Julian, whose cousin and foster-sister, Camilla, has been wedded to his friend and rival, Lionel, endeavours to narrate the story of his own love for her, and the strange sequel of it. He speaks of having been haunted in delirium by visions and the sound of bells, sometimes tolling for a funeral, and at last ringing for a marriage; but he breaks away, overcome, as he approaches the Event, and a witness to it completes the tale.]

* * * * *

HE flies the event: he leaves the event to me:
Poor Julian—how he rush'd away; the bells,
Those marriage bells, echoing in ear and heart—
But cast a parting glance at me, you saw,
As who should say "continue." Well, he had
One golden hour—of triumph shall I say?
Solace at least—before he left his home.

Would you had seen him in that hour of his!

He moved thro' all of it majestically—
Restrain'd himself quite to the close—but now—

   Whether they *were* his lady's marriage-bells,
Or prophets of them in his fantasy,
I never ask'd: but Lionel and the girl
Were wedded, and our Julian came again
Back to his mother's house among the pines.
But there, their gloom, the mountains and the Bay,
The whole land weigh'd him down as Ætna does
The Giant of Mythology: he would go,
Would leave the land for ever, and had gone
Surely, but for a whisper "Go not yet,"
Some warning, and divinely as it seem'd
By that which follow'd—but of this I deem
As of the visions that he told—the event
Glanced back upon them in his after life,
And partly made them—tho' he knew it not.

And thus he stay'd and would not look at her—
No not for months: but, when the eleventh moon
After their marriage lit the lover's Bay,
Heard yet once more the tolling bell, and said,
Would you could toll me out of life, but found—
All softly as his mother broke it to him—
A crueller reason than a crazy-ear,
For that low knell tolling his lady dead—
Dead—and had lain three days without a pulse:
All that look'd on her had pronounced her dead.
And so they bore her (for in Julian's land
They never nail a dumb head up in elm),
Bore her free-faced to the free airs of heaven,
And laid her in the vault of her own kin.

What did he then? not die: he is here and hale—
Not plunge headforemost from the mountain there,
And leave the name of Lover's Leap: not he:

He knew the meaning of the whisper now,
Thought that he knew it. "This, I stay'd for this;
O love, I have not seen you for so long.
Now, now, will I go down into the grave,
I will be all alone with all I love,
And kiss her on the lips. She is his no more:
The dead returns to me, and I go down
To kiss the dead."

      The fancy stirr'd him so
He rose and went, and entering the dim vault,
And, making there a sudden light, beheld
All round about him that which all will be.
The light was but a flash, and went again.
Then at the far end of the vault he saw
His lady with the moonlight on her face;
Her breast as in a shadow-prison, bars
Of black and bands of silver, which the moon

Struck from an open grating overhead
High in the wall, and all the rest of her
Drown'd in the gloom and horror of the vault.

"It was my wish," he said, "to pass, to sleep,
To rest, to be with her—till the great day
Peal'd on us with that music which rights all,
And raised us hand in hand." And kneeling there
Down in the dreadful dust that once was man,
Dust, as he said, that once was loving hearts,
Hearts that had beat with such a love as mine—
Not such as mine, no, nor for such as her—
He softly put his arm about her neck
And kiss'd her more than once, till helpless death
And silence made him bold—nay, but I wrong him,
He reverenced his dear lady even in death;
But, placing his true hand upon her heart,
"O, you warm heart," he moan'd, "not even death

Can chill you all at once:" then starting, thought
His dreams had come again. "Do I wake or sleep?
Or am I made immortal, or my love
Mortal once more?" It beat—the heart—it beat:
Faint—but it beat: at which his own began
To pulse with such a vehemence that it drown'd
The feebler motion underneath his hand.
But when at last his doubts were satisfied,
He raised her softly from the sepulchre,
And, wrapping her all over with the cloak
He came in, and now striding fast, and now
Sitting awhile to rest, but evermore
Holding his golden burthen in his arms,
So bore her thro' the solitary land
Back to the mother's house where she was born.

   There the good mother's kindly ministering,
With half a night's appliances, recall'd

Her fluttering life: she raised an eye that ask'd
"Where?" till the things familiar to her youth
Had made a silent answer: then she spoke,
"Here! and how came I here?" and learning it
(They told her somewhat rashly as I think)
At once began to wander and to wail,
"Ay, but you know that you must give me back:
Send! bid him come;" but Lionel was away
Stung by his loss had vanish'd, none knew where.
"He casts me out," she wept, "and goes"—a wail
That seeming something, yet was nothing, born
Not from believing mind, but shatter'd nerve,
Yet haunting Julian, as her own reproof
At some precipitance in her burial.
Then, when her own true spirit had return'd,
"O yes, and you," she said, "and none but you.
For you have given me life and love again,
And none but you yourself shall tell him of it,

And you shall give me back when he returns."
"Stay then a little," answer'd Julian, "here,
And keep yourself, none knowing, to yourself;
And I will do your will. I may not stay,
No, not an hour; but send me notice of him
When he returns, and then will I return,
And I will make a solemn offering of you
To him you love." And faintly she replied,
"And I will do *your* will, and none shall know."

Not know? with such a secret to be known.
But all their house was old and loved them
        both,
And all the house had known the loves of both;
Had died almost to serve them any way,
And all the land was waste and solitary:
And then he rode away; but after this,
An hour or two, Camilla's travail came

Upon her, and that day a boy was born,
Heir of his face and land, to Lionel.

And thus our lonely lover rode away,
And pausing at a hostel in a marsh,
There fever seized upon him: myself was then
Travelling that land, and meant to rest an hour;
And sitting down to such a base repast,
It makes me angry yet to speak of it—
I heard a groaning overhead, and climb'd
The moulder'd stairs (for everything was vile)
And in a loft, with none to wait on him,
Found, as it seem'd, a skeleton alone,
Raving of dead men's dust and beating hearts.

A dismal hostel in a dismal land,
A flat malarian world of reed and rush!
But there from fever and my care of him

Sprang up a friendship that may help us yet.
For while we roam'd along the dreary coast,
And waited for her message, piece by piece
I learnt the drearier story of his life;
And, tho' he loved and honour'd Lionel,
Found that the sudden wail his lady made
Dwelt in his fancy: did he know her worth,
Her beauty even? should he not be taught,
Ev'n by the price that others set upon it,
The value of that jewel he had to guard?

Suddenly came her notice and we past,
I with our lover to his native Bay.

This love is of the brain, the mind, the soul:
That makes the sequel pure; tho' some of us
Beginning at the sequel know no more.
Not such am I: and yet I say, the bird

That will not hear my call, however sweet,
But if my neighbour whistle answers him—
What matter? there are others in the wood.
Yet when I saw her (and I thought him crazed,
Tho' not with such a craziness as needs
A cell and keeper), those dark eyes of hers—
Oh! such dark eyes! and not her eyes alone,
But all from these to where she touch'd on earth,
For such a craziness as Julian's seem'd
No less than one divine apology.

So sweetly and so modestly she came
To greet us, her young hero in her arms!
"Kiss him," she said. "You gave me life again.
He, but for you, had never seen it once.
His other father you! Kiss him, and then
Forgive him, if his name be Julian too."

Talk of lost hopes and broken heart! his own
Sent such a flame into his face, I knew
Some sudden vivid pleasure hit him there.

But he was all the more resolved to go,
And sent at once to Lionel, praying him
By that great love they both had borne the dead,
To come and revel for one hour with him
Before he left the land for evermore;
And then to friends—they were not many—who lived
Scatteringly about that lonely land of his,
And bade them to a banquet of farewells.

And Julian made a solemn feast: I never
Sat at a costlier; for all round his hall
From column on to column, as in a wood,
Not such as here—an equatorial one,
Great garlands swung and blossom'd; and beneath,

Heirlooms, and ancient miracles of Art,
Chalice and salver, wines that, Heaven knows when,
Had suck'd the fire of some forgotten sun,
And kept it thro' a hundred years of gloom,
Yet glowing in a heart of ruby—cups
Where nymph and god ran ever round in gold—
Others of glass as costly—some with gems
Moveable and resettable at will,
And trebling all the rest in value—Ah heavens!
Why need I tell you all?—suffice to say
That whatsoever such a house as his,
And his was old, has in it rare or fair
Was brought before the guest: and they, the guests,
Wonder'd at some strange light in Julian's eyes
(I told you that he had his golden hour),
And such a feast, ill-suited as it seem'd
To such a time, to Lionel's loss and his,
And that resolved self-exile from a land

He never would revisit, such a feast
So rich, so strange, and stranger ev'n than rich,
But rich as for the nuptials of a king.

And stranger yet, at one end of the hall
Two great funereal curtains, looping down,
Parted a little ere they met the floor,
About a picture of his lady, taken
Some years before, and falling hid the frame.
And just above the parting was a lamp:
So the sweet figure folded round with night
Seem'd stepping out of darkness with a smile

Well then—our solemn feast—we ate and drank,
And might—the wines being of such nobleness—
Have jested also, but for Julian's eyes,
And something weird and wild about it all:
What was it? for our lover seldom spoke,

Scarce touch'd the meats; but ever and anon
A priceless goblet with a priceless wine
Arising, show'd he drank beyond his use;
And when the feast was near an end, he said:

"There is a custom in the Orient, friends—
I read of it in Persia—when a man
Will honour those who feast with him, he brings
And shows them whatsoever he accounts
Of all his treasures the most beautiful,
Gold, jewels, arms, whatever it may be.
This custom—"

                      Pausing here a moment, all
The guests broke in upon him with meeting hands
And cries about the banquet—"Beautiful!
Who could desire more beauty at a feast?"

The lover answer'd, "There is more than one
Here sitting who desires it. Laud me not
Before my time, but hear me to the close.
This custom steps yet further when the guest
Is loved and honour'd to the uttermost.
For after he has shown him gems or gold,
He brings and sets before him in rich guise
That which is thrice as beautiful as these,
The beauty that is dearest to his heart—
'O my heart's lord, would I could show you,' he says,
'Ev'n my heart too.' And I propose to-night
To show you what is dearest to my heart,
And my heart too.

     "But solve me first a doubt.
I knew a man, nor many years ago;
He had a faithful servant, one who loved
His master more than all on earth beside.
He falling sick, and seeming close on death,

His master would not wait until he died,
But bade his menials bear him from the door,
And leave him in the public way to die.
I knew another, not so long ago,
Who found the dying servant, took him home,
And fed, and cherish'd him, and saved his life.
I ask you now, should this first master claim
His service, whom does it belong to? him
Who thrust him out, or him who saved his life?"

This question, so flung down before the guests,
And balanced either way by each, at length
When some were doubtful how the law would hold,
Was handed over by consent of all
To one who had not spoken, Lionel.

Fair speech was his, and delicate of phrase.
And he beginning languidly—his loss

Weigh'd on him yet—but warming as he went,
Glanced at the point of law, to pass it by,
Affirming that as long as either lived,
By all the laws of love and gratefulness,
The service of the one so saved was due
All to the saver—adding, with a smile,
The first for many weeks—a semi-smile
As at a strong conclusion—"body and soul
And life and limbs, all his to work his will."

Then Julian made a secret sign to me
To bring Camilla down before them all.
And crossing her own picture as she came,
And looking as much lovelier than herself
Is lovelier than all others—on her head
A diamond circlet, and from under this
A veil, that seem'd no more than gilded air,
Flying by each fine ear, an Eastern gauze

With seeds of gold—so, with that grace of hers,
Slow-moving as a wave against the wind,
That flings a mist behind it in the sun—
And bearing high in arms the mighty babe,
The younger Julian, who himself was crown'd
With roses, none so rosy as himself—
And over all her babe and her the jewels
Of many generations of his house
Sparkled and flash'd, for he had decked them out
As for a solemn sacrifice of love—
So she came in:—I am long in telling it.
I never yet beheld a thing so strange,
Sad, sweet, and strange together—floated in,—
While all the guests in mute amazement rose,—
And slowly pacing to the middle hall,
Before the board, there paused and stood, her breast
Hard-heaving, and her eyes upon her feet,
Not daring yet to glance at Lionel.

But him she carried, him nor lights nor feast
Dazed or amazed, nor eyes of men; who cared
Only to use his own, and staring wide
And hungering for the gilt and jewell'd world
About him, look'd, as he is like to prove,
When Julian goes, the lord of all he saw.

"My guests," said Julian: "you are honour'd now
Ev'n to the uttermost: in her behold
Of all my treasures the most beautiful,
Of all things upon earth the dearest to me."
Then waving us a sign to seat ourselves,
Led his dear lady to a chair of state.
And I, by Lionel sitting, saw his face
Fire, and dead ashes and all fire again
Thrice in a second, felt him tremble too,
And heard him muttering, "So like, so like;
She never had a sister. I knew none.

Some cousin of his and hers—O God, so like!"
And then he suddenly ask'd her if she were.
She shook, and cast her eyes down, and was dumb.
And then some other question'd if she came
From foreign lands, and still she did not speak.
Another, if the boy were hers: but she
To all their queries answer'd not a word,
Which made the amazement more, till one of them
Said, shuddering, "Her spectre?" But his friend
Replied, in half a whisper, "Not at least
The spectre that will speak if spoken to.
Terrible pity, if one so beautiful
Prove, as I almost dread to find her, dumb!"

But Julian, sitting by her, answer'd all:
"She is but dumb, because in her you see
That faithful servant whom we spoke about,
Obedient to her second master now;

Which will not last. I have here to-night a guest
So bound to me by common love and loss—
What! shall I bind him more? in his behalf,
Shall I exceed the Persian, giving him
That which of all things is the dearest to me,
Not only showing? and he himself pronounced
That my rich gift is wholly mine to give.

"Now all be dumb, and promise all of you
Not to break in on what I say by word
Or whisper, while I show you all my heart."
And then began the story of his love
As here to-day, but not so wordily—
The passionate moment would not suffer that—
Past thro' his visions to the burial; thence
Down to this last strange hour in his own hall;
And then rose up, and with him all his guests
Once more as by enchantment; all but he,

Lionel, who fain had risen, but fell again,
And sat as if in chains—to whom he said:

"Take my free gift, my cousin, for your wife;
And were it only for the giver's sake,
And tho' she seem so like the one you lost,
Yet cast her not away so suddenly,
Lest there be none left here to bring her back:
I leave this land for ever." Here he ceased.

Then taking his dear lady by one hand,
And bearing on one arm the noble babe,
He slowly brought them both to Lionel.
And there the widower husband and dead wife
Rush'd each at each with a cry, that rather seem'd
For some new death than for a life renew'd;
At this the very babe began to wail;
At once they turn'd, and caught and brought him in

To their charm'd circle, and, half-killing him
With kisses, round him closed and claspt again.
But Lionel, when at last he freed himself
From wife and child, and lifted up a face
All over glowing with the sun of life,
And love, and boundless thanks—the sight of this
So frighted our good friend, that turning to me
And saying, "It is over: let us go"—
There were our horses ready at the doors—
We bade them no farewell, but mounting these
He past for ever from his native land;
And I with him, my Julian, back to mine.

THE VICTIM.

I.

A PLAGUE upon the people fell,
   A famine after laid them low,
Then thorpe and byre arose in fire,
   For on them brake the sudden foe;
So thick they died the people cried
   "The Gods are moved against the land."
The Priest in horror about his altar
   To Thor and Odin lifted a hand:

"Help us from famine
And plague and strife!
What would you have of us?
Human life?
Were it our nearest,
Were it our dearest,
(Answer, O answer)
We give you his life."

II.

But still the foeman spoil'd and burn'd,
  And cattle died, and deer in wood,
And bird in air, and fishes turn'd
  And whiten'd all the rolling flood;
And dead men lay all over the way,
  Or down in a furrow scathed with flame:
And ever and aye the Priesthood moan'd
  Till at last it seem'd that an answer came:

"The King is happy
In child and wife;
Take you his dearest,
Give us a life,"

III.

The Priest went out by heath and hill;
 The King was hunting in the wild;
They found the mother sitting still;
 She cast her arms about the child.
The child was only eight summers old,
 His beauty still with his years increased,
His face was ruddy, his hair was gold,
 He seem'd a victim due to the priest.
  The Priest beheld him,
  And cried with joy,
  "The Gods have answer'd:
  We give them the boy."

IV.

The King return'd from out the wild,
  He bore but little game in hand;
The mother said "They have taken the child
  To spill his blood and heal the land:
The land is sick, the people diseased,
  And blight and famine on all the lea:
The holy Gods, they must be appeased,
  So I pray you tell the truth to me.
      They have taken our son,
      They will have his life.
      Is *he* your dearest?
      Or I, the wife?"

V.

The King bent low, with hand on brow,
  He stay'd his arms upon his knee:
"O wife, what use to answer now?
  For now the Priest has judged for me."

The King was shaken with holy fear;
  "The Gods," he said, "would have chosen well;
Yet both are near, and both are dear,
  And which the dearest I cannot tell!"
    But the Priest was happy,
    His victim won:
    "We have his dearest,
    His only son!"

VI.

The rites prepared, the victim bared,
  The knife uprising toward the blow,
To the altar-stone she sprang alone,
  "Me, not my darling, no!"
He caught her away with a sudden cry;
  Suddenly from him brake his wife,
And shrieking "*I* am his dearest, I—
  I am his dearest!" rush'd on the knife.

And the Priest was happy,
"O, Father Odin,
We give you a life.
Which was his nearest?
Who was his dearest?
The Gods have answer'd;
We give them the wife!"

WAGES.

Glory of warrior, glory of orator, glory of song,
  Paid with a voice flying by to be lost on an endless sea—
Glory of Virtue, to fight, to struggle, to right the wrong—
  Nay, but she aim'd not at glory, no lover of glory she:
Give her the glory of going on, and still to be.

The wages of sin is death: if the wages of Virtue be dust,
Would she have heart to endure for the life of the worm and the fly?
She desires no isles of the blest, no quiet seats of the just,
To rest in a golden grove, or to bask in a summer sky:
Give her the wages of going on, and not to die.

THE HIGHER PANTHEISM.

THE sun, the moon, the stars, the seas, the hills and the plains—
Are not these, O Soul, the Vision of Him who reigns?

Is not the Vision He? tho' He be not that which He seems?
Dreams are true while they last, and do we not live in dreams?

Earth, these solid stars, this weight of body and limb,
Are they not sign and symbol of thy division from
Him?

Dark is the world to thee: thyself art the reason
why;
For is He not all but thou, that hast power to feel
"I am I?"

Glory about thee, without thee; and thou fulfillest
thy doom,
Making Him broken gleams, and a stifled splendour
and gloom.

Speak to Him thou for He hears, and Spirit with
Spirit can meet—
Closer is He than breathing, and nearer than hands
and feet.

THE HIGHER PANTHEISM.

God is law, say the wise; O Soul, and let us rejoice,
For if He thunder by law the thunder is yet His voice.

Law is God, say some: no God at all, says the fool;
For all we have power to see is a straight staff bent in a pool;

And the ear of man cannot hear, and the eye of man cannot see;
But if we could see and hear, this Vision—were it not He?

FLOWER in the crannied wall,
I pluck you out of the crannies;—
Hold you here, root and all, in my hand,
Little flower—but if I could understand
What you are, root and all, and all in all,
I should know what God and man is.

LUCRETIUS.

LUCILIA, wedded to Lucretius, found
Her master cold; for when the morning flush
Of passion and the first embrace had died
Between them, tho' he loved her none the less,
Yet often when the woman heard his foot
Return from pacings in the field, and ran
To greet him with a kiss, the master took
Small notice, or austerely, for—his mind
Half buried in some weightier argument,
Or fancy-borne perhaps upon the rise
And long roll of the Hexameter—he past

To turn and ponder those three hundred scrolls
Left by the Teacher whom he held divine.
She brook'd it not; but wrathful, petulant,
Dreaming some rival, sought and found a witch
Who brew'd the philtre which had power, they said,
To lead an errant passion home again.
And this, at times, she mingled with his drink,
And this destroy'd him; for the wicked broth
Confused the chemic labour of the blood,
And tickling the brute brain within the man's
Made havock among those tender cells, and check'd
His power to shape: he loath'd himself; and once
After a tempest woke upon a morn
That mock'd him with returning calm, and cried;

"Storm in the night! for thrice I heard the rain
Rushing; and once the flash of a thunderbolt—
Methought I never saw so fierce a fork—

Struck out the streaming mountain-side, and show'd
A riotous confluence of watercourses
Blanching and billowing in a hollow of it,
Where all but yester-eve was dusty-dry.

"Storm, and what dreams, ye holy Gods, what dreams!
For thrice I waken'd after dreams. Perchance
We do but recollect the dreams that come
Just ere the waking: terrible! for it seem'd
A void was made in Nature; all her bonds
Crack'd; and I saw the flaring atom streams
And torrents of her myriad universe,
Ruining along the illimitable inane,
Fly on to clash together again, and make
Another and another frame of things
For ever: that was mine, my dream, I knew it—
Of and belonging to me, as the dog

With inward yelp and restless forefoot plies
His function of the woodland: but the next!
I thought that all the blood by Sylla shed
Came driving rainlike down again on earth,
And where it dash'd the reddening meadow, sprang
No dragon warriors from Cadmean teeth,
For these I thought my dream would show to me,
But girls, Hetairai, curious in their art,
Hired animalisms, vile as those that made
The mulberry-faced Dictator's orgies worse
Than aught they fable of the quiet Gods.
And hands they mixt, and yell'd and round me drove
In narrowing circles till I yell'd again
Half-suffocated, and sprang up, and saw—
Was it the first beam of my latest day?

"Then, then, from utter gloom stood out the breasts,

The breasts of Helen, and hoveringly a sword
Now over and now under, now direct,
Pointed itself to pierce, but sank down shamed
At all that beauty; and as I stared, a fire,
The fire that left a roofless Ilion,
Shot out of them, and scorch'd me that I woke.

"Is this thy vengeance, holy Venus, thine,
Because I would not one of thine own doves,
Not ev'n a rose, were offer'd to thee? thine,
Forgetful how my rich procemion makes
Thy glory fly along the Italian field,
In lays that will outlast thy Deity?

"Deity? nay, thy worshippers. My tongue
Trips, or I speak profanely. Which of these
Angers thee most, or angers thee at all?
Not if thou be'st of those who, far aloof

From envy, hate and pity, and spite and scorn,
Live the great life which all our greatest fain
Would follow, center'd in eternal calm.

"Nay, if thou can'st, O Goddess, like ourselves
Touch, and be touch'd, then would I cry to thee
To kiss thy Mavors, roll thy tender arms
Round him, and keep him from the lust of blood
That makes a steaming slaughter-house of Rome.

"Ay, but I meant not thee; I meant not her,
Whom all the pines of Ida shook to see
Slide from that quiet heaven of hers, and tempt
The Trojan, while his neat-herds were abroad;
Nor her that o'er her wounded hunter wept
Her Deity false in human-amorous tears;
Nor whom her beardless apple-arbiter
Decided fairest. Rather, O ye Gods,

Poet-like, as the great Sicilian called
Calliope to grace his golden verse—
Ay, and this Kypris also—did I take
That popular name of thine to shadow forth
The all-generating powers and genial heat
Of Nature, when she strikes thro' the thick blood
Of cattle, and light is large, and lambs are glad
Nosing the mother's udder, and the bird
Makes his heart voice amid the blaze of flowers:
Which things appear the work of mighty Gods.

"The Gods! and if I go *my* work is left
Unfinish'd—*if* I go. The Gods, who haunt
The lucid interspace of world and world,
Where never creeps a cloud, or moves a wind,
Nor ever falls the least white star of snow,
Nor ever lowest roll of thunder moans,
Nor sound of human sorrow mounts to mar

Their sacred everlasting calm! and such,
Not all so fine, nor so divine a calm,
Not such, nor all unlike it, man may gain
Letting his own life go. The Gods, the Gods!
If all be atoms, how then should the Gods
Being atomic not be dissoluble,
Not follow the great law? My master held
That Gods there are, for all men so believe.
I prest my footsteps into his, and meant
Surely to lead my Memmius in a train
Of flowery clauses onward to the proof
That Gods there are, and deathless. Meant? I meant?
I have forgotten what I meant: my mind
Stumbles, and all my faculties are lamed.

"Look where another of our Gods, the Sun,
Apollo, Delius, or of older use
All-seeing Hyperion—what you will—

Has mounted yonder; since he never sware,
Except his wrath were wreak'd on wretched man,
That he would only shine among the dead
Hereafter; tales! for never yet on earth
Could dead flesh creep, or bits of roasting ox
Moan round the spit—nor knows he what he sees;
King of the East altho' he seem, and girt
With song and flame and fragrance, slowly lifts
His golden feet on those empurpled stairs
That climb into the windy halls of heaven:
And here he glances on an eye new-born,
And gets for greeting but a wail of pain;
And here he stays upon a freezing orb
That fain would gaze upon him to the last;
And here upon a yellow eyelid fall'n
And closed by those who mourn a friend in vain,
Not thankful that his troubles are no more.
And me, altho' his fire is on my face

Blinding, he sees not, nor at all can tell
Whether I mean this day to end myself,
Or lend an ear to Plato where he says,
That men like soldiers may not quit the post
Allotted by the Gods: but he that holds
The Gods are careless, wherefore need he care
Greatly for them, nor rather plunge at once,
Being troubled, wholly out of sight, and sink
Past earthquake—ay, and gout and stone, that break
Body toward death, and palsy, death-in-life,
And wretched age—and worst disease of all,
These prodigies of myriad nakednesses,
And twisted shapes of lust, unspeakable,
Abominable, strangers at my hearth
Not welcome, harpies miring every dish,
The phantom husks of something foully done,
And fleeting thro' the boundless universe,

And blasting the long quiet of my breast
With animal heat and dire insanity?

"How should the mind, except it loved them, clasp
These idols to herself? or do they fly
Now thinner, and now thicker, like the flakes
In a fall of snow, and so press in, perforce
Of multitude, as crowds that in an hour
Of civic tumult jam the doors, and bear
The keepers down, and throng, their rags and they,
The basest, far into that council-hall
Where sit the best and stateliest of the land?

"Can I not fling this horror off me again,
Seeing with how great ease Nature can smile,
Balmier and nobler from her bath of storm,
At random ravage? and how easily

The mountain there has cast his cloudy slough,
Now towering o'er him in serenest air,
A mountain o'er a mountain,—ay and within
All hollow as the hopes and fears of men?

"But who was he, that in the garden snared
Picus and Faunus, rustic Gods? a tale
To laugh at—more to laugh at in myself—
For look! what is it? there? yon arbutus
Totters; a noiseless riot underneath
Strikes through the wood, sets all the tops quiver-
      ing—
The mountain quickens into Nymph and Faun;
And here an Oread—how the sun delights
To glance and shift about her slippery sides,
And rosy knees and supple roundedness,
And budded bosom-peaks—who this way runs
Before the rest—A satyr, a satyr, see,

Follows; but him I proved impossible;
Twy-natured is no nature; yet he draws
Nearer and nearer, and I scan him now
Beastlier than any phantom of his kind
That ever butted his rough brother-brute
For lust or lusty blood or provender:
I hate, abhor, spit, sicken at him; and she
Loathes him as well; such a precipitate heel,
Fledged as it were with Mercury's ankle-wing,
Whirls her to me: but will she fling herself,
Shameless upon me? Catch her, goatfoot: nay,
Hide, hide them, million-myrtled wilderness,
And cavern-shadowing laurels, hide! do I wish—
What?—that the bush were leafless? or to whelm
All of them in one massacre? O ye Gods,
I know you careless, yet, behold, to you
From childly wont and ancient use I call—
I thought I lived securely as yourselves—

No lewdness, narrowing envy, monkey-spite,
No madness of ambition, avarice, none:
No larger feast than under plane or pine
With neighbours laid along the grass, to take
Only such cups as left us friendly-warm,
Affirming each his own philosophy—
Nothing to mar the sober majesties
Of settled, sweet, Epicurean life.
But now it seems some unseen monster lays
His vast and filthy hands upon my will,
Wrenching it backward into his; and spoils
My bliss in being; and it was not great;
For save when shutting reasons up in rhythm,
Or Heliconian honey in living words,
To make a truth less harsh, I often grew
Tired of so much within our little life,
Or of so little in our little life—
Poor little life that toddles half an hour

Crown'd with a flower or two, and there an end—
And since the nobler pleasure seems to fade,
Why should I, beastlike as I find myself,
Not manlike end myself?—our privilege—
What beast has heart to do it? And what man,
What Roman would be dragg'd in triumph thus?
Not I; not he, who bears one name with her
Whose death-blow struck the dateless doom of
   kings,
When, brooking not the Tarquin in her veins,
She made her blood in sight of Collatine
And all his peers, flushing the guiltless air,
Spout from the maiden fountain in her heart.
And from it sprang the Commonwealth, which breaks
As I am breaking now!

     "And therefore now
Let her, that is the womb and tomb of all,

Great Nature, take, and forcing far apart
Those blind beginnings that have made me man
Dash them anew together at her will
Through all her cycles—into man once more,
Or beast or bird or fish, or opulent flower:
But till this cosmic order everywhere
Shatter'd into one earthquake in one day
Cracks all to pieces,—and that hour perhaps
Is not so far when momentary man
Shall seem no more a something to himself,
But he, his hopes and hates, his homes and fanes,
And even his bones long laid within the grave,
The very sides of the grave itself shall pass,
Vanishing, atom and void, atom and void,
Into the unseen for ever,—till that hour,
My golden work in which I told a truth
That stays the rolling Ixionian wheel,
And numbs the Fury's ringlet-snake, and plucks

The mortal soul from out immortal hell,
Shall stand: ay, surely: then it fails at last
And perishes as I must; for O Thou,
Passionless bride, divine Tranquillity,
Yearn'd after by the wisest of the wise,
Who fail to find thee, being as thou art
Without one pleasure and without one pain,
Howbeit I know thou surely must be mine
Or soon or late, yet out of season, thus
I woo thee roughly, for thou carest not
How roughly men may woo thee so they win—
Thus—thus: the soul flies out and dies in the air."

With that he drove the knife into his side:
She heard him raging, heard him fall; ran in,
Beat breast, tore hair, cried out upon herself
As having fail'd in duty to him, shriek'd
That she but meant to win him back, fell on him,

Clasp'd, kiss'd him, wail'd: he answer'd, "Care not
    thou!
Thy duty! What is duty! Fare thee well!"

END OF VOL. VI.

www.ingramcontent.com/pod-product-compliance
Lightning Source LLC
Chambersburg PA
CBHW021831230426
43669CB00008B/932